Sefer
Newly Born Jew
Noahides & Conversion to Judaism

Written by
Reb Moshe Steinerman

Edited by Rochel Steinerman

Ilovetorah Jewish Outreach Network

Ilovetorah Jewish Publishing
First Published 2019
ISBN: 978-1-947706-09-5

Copyright: ilovetorah Jewish Publishing
www.ilovetorah.com
moshe@ilovetorah.com

All Rights reserved

Editor: Rochel Steinerman

ABOUT THE AUTHOR

Rabbi Moshe Steinerman grew up as a religious Jew on the hillsides of Maryland. During his teenage years, Reb Moshe developed his talent for photography, while connecting to nature and speaking to Hashem. He later found his path through Breslav *Chassidus*, while maintaining closeness to the *Litvish* style of learning. He studied in the Baltimore *yeshiva*, Ner Yisrael; then married and moved to Lakewood, New Jersey. After settling down, he began to write Kavanos Halev, with the blessing of Rav Malkiel Kotler Shlita, Rosh Yeshiva of Beis Medresh Gevoah.

After establishing one of the first Jewish outreach websites, IloveTorah.com in 1996, Reb Moshe's teachings became popular among the full spectrum of Jews, from the unaffiliated to ultra-Orthodox. His teachings, including hundreds of stories of *tzaddikim*, gained popularity due to the ideal of drawing Jews together. Reb Moshe made aliyah to Tzfat in 2003 and since then has been helping English-speaking Jews to return to Judaism through his popular Jewish videos and audio shiurim. His learning experience includes the completion of both Talmud Bavli and Yerushalmi as well as other important works.

In 2012, Reb Moshe, with his wife and children, moved to Jerusalem. Some of his other books are Kavanos Halev (Meditations of the Heart), Tikkun Shechinah, Tovim Meoros (Glimpse of Light), Yom Leyom (Day by Day), Chassidus, Kabbalah & Meditation, Prayers of the Heart, Pesukei Torah (Passages of Torah), Pathways of the Righteous, A Journey into Holiness, and The True Intentions of the Baal Shem Tov. Thousands have read the advice contained in these books, with life-changing results.

In Memory of my father Shlomo Zavel Ben Yaakov ZT"L My father-in-law Menachem Ben Reuven ZT"L And all the great souls of our people

I grew up in a house filled with the Torah learning of my father, who studied most of the day. Although there were no Jews in this remote part of Maryland, my father was a man of chesed to all people and was known for his brilliance in Torah scholarship.

In Memory of My grandparents Yaakov Ben Shmuel Zavel, Toba Esther bas Gedalya Aharon Hakohein, Yehudah ben Ike, Isabella Bas Israel My great-grandmother Nechama bas Sara Rivka, My Uncle Shmuel Yosef ben Gedalya Aharon Hakohein

I want to say a special thank you to the Nikolsberg Rebbe and the Biala Rebbe for their encouragement and blessings. Most of all, I offer thanks to my wife, Rochel, for her faithful support.

*Dedicated to my wife Rochel
and to my children Shlomo Nachman, Yaakov Yosef,
Gedalya Aharon Tzvi, Esther Rivka, Yeshiya Michel,
Dovid Shmuel, Eliyahu Yisrael
may it bring forth the light of your neshamos.*

Dear Reader,

Ilovetorah Jewish Outreach is a non-profit and books and Torah classes are available at low costs. Therefore, we appreciate your donation to help Rabbi Moshe Steinerman and ilovetorah.com to continue their work on behalf of the Jewish people. We also ask that you pass on these books to others once you are finished with them.

Thank you,
Reb Moshe Steinerman
www.ilovetorah.com/donations

RABBINIC APPROVALS / HASKAMOS

בס״ד

RABBI DOVID B. KAPLAN
RABBI OF WEST NEW YORK
5308 PALISADE AVENUE • WEST NEW YORK, NJ 07093
201-867-6859 • WESTNEWYORKSHUL@GMAIL.COM

דוד ברוך הלוי קאפלאן
רב ואב״ד דק״ק
וועסט ניו יארק

י' שבט ה'תשע"ז / February 6, 2017

Dear Friends,

Shalom and Blessings!

For approximately twenty years I have followed the works of Rabbi Moshe Steinerman, Shlit"a, a pioneer in the use of social media to encourage people and bring them closer to G-d.

Over the years Rabbi Steinerman has produced, and made public at no charge, hundreds of videos sharing his Torah wisdom, his holy stories, and his touching songs. Rabbi Steinerman has written a number of books, all promoting true Jewish Torah spirituality. Rabbi Steinerman's works have touched many thousands of Jews, and even spirituality-seeking non-Jews, from all walks of life and at all points of the globe.

Rabbi Steinerman is a tomim (pure-hearted one) in the most flattering sense of the word.

I give my full approbation and recommendation to all of Rabbi Steinerman's works.

I wish Rabbi Steinerman much success in all his endeavors.

May G-d bless Rabbi Moshe Steinerman, his wife, Rebbetzin Rochel Steinerman, and their beautiful children; and may G-d grant them health, success, and nachas!

With blessings,

Rabbi Dovid B. Kaplan

הובא לפני גליונות בעניני קירוב רחוקים לקרב אחינו בני ישראל אל
אביהם שבשמים, כידוע מהבעש"ט זיע"א שאמר "אימתי קאתי מר
לכשיפוצו מעינותיך חוצה" ואפריון נמטי"ה להאי גברא יקירא מיקירי
צפת עיה"ק תובב"א כמע"כ מוהר"ר משה שטיינרמן שליט"א אשר כבר
עוסק רבות בשנים לקרב רחוקים לתורה וליהדות, וכעת מוציא לאור
ספר בשם "יהודי שנולד מחדש" וראיתי דברים נחמדים מאוד וניכר מתוך
הדברים שהרב בעל המחבר - אהבת השי"ת ואהבת התורה וישראל
בלבבו, ובטחוני כי הספר יביא תועלת גדולה לכל עם ישראל.

ויה"ר שיזכה לבוא לגומרה ברוב פאר והדר ונזכה לגאולתן של ישראל
בב"א.

בכבוד רב:
אהרן שלמה חיים אליעזר
בלאאו"ר הגה"ה ה אבי'אלא

Approval of the Biala Rebbe of New York / Beitar / Miami

Reb Moshe Steinerman

Rabbi M. Lebovits

Grand Rabbi of
Nikolsburg

53 Decatur Avenue
Spring Valley, N.Y. 10977

יוסף יחיאל מיכל
לעבאוויטש
ניקלשבורג

מאנסי - ספרינג וואלי, נ.י.

בעזהשי"ת

בשורותי אלו באתי להעיד על מעשה אומן, מופלא מופלג בהפלגת חכמים ונבונים,
ירא וחרד לדבר ה', ומשתוקק לקרב לבות ישראל לאביהם שבשמים,
ה"ה הרב **משה שטיינערמאן** שליט"א בעיה"ק צפת תובב"א

שעלה בידו להעלות על הספר דברים נפלאים שאסף מספרים הקדושים, בענין אהבה
אחוה שלום ורעיות, לראות מעלות חברינו ולא חסרונם, ועי"ז להיות נמנעים מדברי
ריבות ומחלוקת, ולתקן עון שנאת חנם אשר בשביל זה נחרב בית מקדשינו
ותפארתינו, וכמשאחז"ל (רש"י, ומיקרא רבה פ' ט) על ויחן שם ישראל, שניתנה תורה באופן
שחנו שם כאיש אחד בלב אחד.

וניכר בספר כי עמל ויגע הרבה להוציא מתח"י דבר נאה ומתוקן, ע"כ אף ידי תכון
עמו להוציאו לאור עולם. ויהי רצון שחפץ ה' בידו יצליח, ויברך ה' חילו ופועל ידו
תרצה, שיברך על המוגמר להגדיל תורה ולהאדירה ולהפיצו בקרב ישראל, עד ביאת
גוא"צ בב"א

א"ד הכותב לכבוד התורה ומרביציה.
י"ט חשון תשס"ו

Rabbi Abraham Y. S. Friedman
161 Maple Avenue #C Spring Valley NY 10977
Tel: 845-425-5043 Fax: 845-425-8045

אברהם יחזקאל שרגא פריעדמאן
רב דביהמ"ד אמר"י שפ"ר קאמאדא
וראש כולל האר"י

בעזהשי"ת

ישפות השם החיים והשלו', לכבוד ידידי מאז ומקדם מיקירי קרתא
דירושלים יראה שלם, זוכה ומזכה אחרים, להיות דבוק באלקינו, ה"ה
הר"ר משה שטיינרמאן שליט"א.

שמחתי מאוד לשמוע ממך, מאתר רחוק וקירוב הלבבות, בעסק
תורתך הקדושה ועבודתך בלי לאות, וכה יעזור ה' להלאה ביתר שאת
ויתר עז. והנה שלחת את הספר שלקטת בעניני דביקות בה', לקרב
לבבות בני ישראל לאבינו שבשמים בשפת אנגלית, אבל דא עקא
השפת לא ידענו, ע"כ לא זכיתי לקרותו, ע"כ א"א לי ליתן הסכמה פרטי
על ספרך, ובכלל קיבלתי על עצמי שלא ליתן הסכמות, ובפרט כשאין
לי פנאי לקרות הספר מתחלתו עד סופו, אבל בכלליות זכרתי לך חסד
נעוריך, היאך ה' המתיקות שלך בעבודת השם פה בעירינו, ובנועם
המדות, וחזקה על חבר שאינו מוציא מתחת ידו דבר שאינו מתוקן,
ובפרט שכל מגמתך להרבות כבוד שמים, שבודאי סייעתא דשמיא
ילוך כל ימיך לראות רב נחת מיוצ"ח ומפרי ידיך, שתתקבל הספר
בסבר פנים יפות אצל אחינו בני ישראל שמדברים בשפת האנגלית
שיתקרבו לאבינו שבשמים ולהדבק בו באמת כאות נפשך, ולהרבות
פעלים לתורה ועבודה וקדושה בדביקות עם מדות טובות, בנייחותא
נייחא בעליונים ונייחא בתחתונים עד ביאת גואל צדק בב"א.

כ"ד ידיד השמח בהצלחתך ובעבודתך

אברהם יחזקאל שרגא פריעדמאן

TABLE OF CONTENTS

OVERVIEW

Judaism is not a religion, there is no such word in the Torah because it is the "Eternal Truth". When the Messiah comes, and those of the nations that remain, will all know that there is ONLY Hashem and no other, *Ein Od Milvado*; for the knowledge of Hashem will fill the earth as the waters cover the seas.

Religion is a belief system made up by people. There are approximately 4,200 religions in the world, but only one system that came from the Creator, therefore, it is not a religion. It is a Divinely given way of life

"Decades ago," wrote my father-in-law Menachem ben Reuven z"l, "when I became a Torah observant Jew people said to me, 'it looks like you discovered a new way of life.' I used to answer: 'No, I discovered life itself.' When you start living the truth you are not in a belief system, but in a world of Devine knowledge. I don't believe in Hashem – I know He exists. I don't believe that Judaism is life – I know it is.

"The substantial difference between now and the time of the Messiah is that now we live in a physical, fantasy world of falsehood. The upside-down world is our daily existence. The time of the Messiah will be a time of truth, a spiritual existence and therefore all made up religions in the world will no longer exist. When the good, righteous people of the world do not believe, but KNOW, of the One Living G-d, everyone will KNOW and LIVE the truth. They will not have to be taught such feelings – it will be as natural as our fantasy world is to us today. Hashem will no longer be hidden, and everyone will know beyond a shadow of a doubt: *Ein Od Milvado*!!!! – There is only Hashem.

"Those who develop the feeling now and start living the absolute truth, even before the Messiah is announced, will be the happiest people of all. Jews and righteous non-Jews who abandon the fantasy world of today, will be able to join the world of truth."

As the time of the Messiah's arrival becomes closer, we see more people than ever wanting to convert to Judaism. They notice that the world around them is slowly falling apart, and they want to hold onto whatever truth they can find. It has become apparent to them that the only truth, is in Judaism.

"Sometimes your soul knows, before your mind, where it needs to go." (Avigail Rivka Hasofer) It could be that inside your heart you just feel that becoming Jewish is the right thing. You may not even be able to explain it to yourself. There is simply a calling and it's for you to go to the extreme in life, forget everything you know and just become Jewish.

One of the greatest things about being Jewish is observing the *Shabbos*. It isn't an accident that other religions seem to observe their own sabbath on a different day, leaving ours to bask in its own holiness. When other nations observe a day of rest, it really can't compare to the Jewish *Shabbos* which is observed in total simplicity and was Divinely given.

My father-in-law writes, "The greatest and most enjoyable improvement when we became more religious, was in our family life. Before we became observant, my wife, two children and I would sit, and watch television together but never realized that we were four people in different worlds and miles apart. We didn't talk to each other or share life together. We only went through motions and pretended to know one another. Suddenly, when we began observing the *Shabbos*, there was no television and distractions. We sat around the dinner table and actually started to talk to each other. We shared Torah issues that we had learned and found ourselves teaching each other. We sang, we laughed and, best of all, we discovered how much we love each other.

"To this day my wife and I couldn't be closer with our children, but to really talk about pure happiness is having grandchildren. Even though we only had two children, we now have 19 grandchildren. The best part is that our children and grandchildren are very good people. They are beautiful, intelligent (bi-lingual), totally respectful and very pleasant to be with (this is an unbiased opinion). They don't fight, they don't argue, and they always help each other. This type of behavior isn't limited to my family. Children that I have met in many observant Jewish communities are the absolute best in the world. The expressions: 'kids will be kids' and 'teenagers will be teenagers' are meaningless to me since they are usually just excuses for misbehaving."

Becoming Jewish is really the best gift you can give to your family. Instead of living the common life that has no real purpose outside your own life, you give them one full of meaning and purpose. There was once a secular Israeli soldier who was injured during the Israel war and while he was laying there wondering if anyone would ever find him alive, the only thing he could think about was observing the holidays with his father. He tried thinking about his many accomplishments and the things that were always important to him but none of them brought him comfort. Only the little observance he kept in Judaism brought him enough comfort to sustain him until he was found and rescued. From that moment on, he decided that if he would be granted a second chance, he would devote it towards providing children with a Jewish education. Soon after he was rescued and became a religious Jew.

The Prophesy says in the book of Zechariah, "Thus said the L-rd of Hosts, 'In those days it shall come to pass that ten men out of all the languages of the nations, shall take hold-yea, they shall take hold of the skirts of him that is a Jew, saying, Let us go with you, for we have heard that G-d is with you.'"

When the Messiah arrives, it will be too late to be accepted to Judaism or to become a B'nei Noach. Only those who already accepted G-d will remain in the world to serve Him. One thing is for certain, you have found this book because you know there is something special about the Jewish nation. You have clearly seen that the world is going nowhere without the holy Jewish people and you have learned to respect them. Now the only question left unanswered is, "Do I, too, become a Jew or remain a Noahide?"

Rabbi Eleazar taught, "The Holy One exiled Israel among the nations, only in order that proselytes might be multiplied among them." (Pesachim 87b)

INTRODUCTION

Why would anyone want to convert to Judaism, and how can a person not consider conversion when Judaism is clearly the most truthful path one can pursue?

In Judaism, we don't go out preaching to other nations to join us as other religious are prone to do. So, it's a wonder that people find us at all and are actually interested in this minority group of ours. What's more to question is, why would anyone consider joining a nation that has only suffered their entire existence? Our suffering is well known and documented.

If we were to list here all the reasons not to convert, it would be quite a long collection. Practically speaking, there are no normal people that convert to Judaism. Therefore, it has to be some sort of internal calling, a spark that can't be explained logically. This calling, if unanswered can be emotionally painful, filled with loneliness, confusion and grief. Therefore, you must address this yearning seriously.

People who are seeking to better understand this calling, usually start out inside the B'nei Noach, Noahide movement, fulfilling the Torah commandments for gentiles. Many might even find themselves in the false messianic Judaism movement which is mostly just a Christian cult used to convert Jews to Christianity. Anything that even has a trace of Judaism seems to spark the interest of the searching non-Jew. G-d protect those lost in such a false movement as Messianic Judaism which believe in Jesus as they secretly call him. Thousands of Jews have been trapped by the snare of these pretend to be Jews. It is quite common for spiritually searching people to get caught up in spiritually fulfilling eastern religions only to latter find them to be lacking any real substance.

The B'nei Noach movement has some wonderful aspects to it. It however has always lacked leadership and unification. This could be why someone might feel they need to convert to Judaism, in order to get a larger spectrum of friends and support, so to speak.

Many years ago, I personally made a social media platform for socializing online as a B'nei Noach. My work was featured on Tuvia

Singer's radio show and many websites. However, the B'nei Noach people didn't seem to stand behind my efforts in a unified way so eventually, it just closed down. This could be because there is not one leader in the Noahide movement. I really don't know if there even could be. The Noahide movement is so filled with diversity, many times it's just a pit stop on the way to becoming Jewish.

There is a lot of work to be done to help the B'nei Noach, and I hope with continued efforts over the years, I can fix many foundational aspects. However, for some, this movement doesn't do enough to complete their yearnings for Judaism.

Often the thirsty Noahides start expanding their observance and adding more and more laws, instead of just the seven required laws. Also, to quench their thirst, they begin to read well beyond the scope of their allowance and branch through all Judaic studies. Even though we can't encourage this to regular B'nei Noach, those with a higher calling, seem to grab whatever Torah they can find in an attempt to feel content. However, this may still not be enough. It could be that inside is a truly Jewish spark that can only be quenched through the lengthy conversion practice.

In order to make a proper conversion Jewish one must commit to all the laws of *Shabbos*, keeping *kosher* and the complete 613 commandments. Rather than overwhelm themselves, the seeker may attempt to take shortcuts through non-orthodox conversion and accepting only the laws they enjoy, leaving out the more difficult ones. This is not how to convert and is certainly not fulfilling the Will of Hashem. The internal pains and struggles to find oneself only continue and a life of emptiness pursues. Only through a total commitment to Judaism, can one receive the higher soul levels of a Jew. However, a person can't force a Jewish soul upon themselves if it wasn't pre-ordained from G-d. Judaism isn't a fix all to your life's problems.

This isn't a religion of shortcuts. If it were, we would seek out newcomers ourselves. The Talmud explains that, "a convert is like a scab on the skin of a person." (Yevamos 47b) His conversion doesn't help to bring the Messiah. That is, a convert who joins without a total commitment can bring more harm to the Jewish nation than good.

Up to one-third of Orthodox converts and two-thirds of Conservative converts choose Judaism to marry a Jew. Someone who converts for ulterior motives such as loving a Jew and wishing to marry them or just to add some extra spirituality to their life, is making a mistake. It is a band aide placed upon a wound without any medicine that soon will be ripped off by the truth, "I am in way over my head." Next thing you know, the person is a questionable convert who barely even keeps the laws of Noach. Do we not have enough Jews who already refuse to keep the basic laws? Are we in need of more?

This book is for true seekers, people willing to make a total commitment to Hashem and the Torah. Should you truly have this calling to become Jewish, with you comes a lot of light, holiness, and responsibility. The Torah teaches us to respect the convert like our own and to embrace them like our own family. "You must understand the feelings of the convert." (Exodus 23:9) Often when it speaks about converts, it also mentions the importance of loving the widow and the orphan. The Torah recognizes all three as being extremely important.

When someone converts, they also convert many holy sparks of holiness that were caught up in impurities and return them back to holiness. Rebbe Nachman teaches that sometimes a holy soul must come down to the world because it is so special that the forces of evil fight for it to not be born. In order to compromise so the soul can descend, the child is given to a family that many not be observant and eventually, that child finds his way back to holy Judaism.

When a born Jew performs the commandments, they too elevate the fallen sparks back into holiness. However, because of this holy Jewish soul, they can't bring back sparks that have fallen deeply into impurity, as a convert is able to because their soul can only go down so far. Even the worst Jewish sinner still has a relevant holiness inside them that is completely connected to all their fellow Jews and Hashem. However, one who wasn't born Jewish, when they find Hashem, with them, elevates all these lower sparks back to their source. "You shall love the convert." (Deuteronomy 10:10) This is one of many reasons why we must respect and love the convert like our own. They have created much light through their returning and the coming of the Messiah is brought closer through their proper conversion. However, this special person isn't always common.

Most converts today never were committed during their conversion process and some were even misled into thinking they converted properly when they hadn't accepted the main requirements of conversion. Instead of drawing more holiness into Judaism, they have polluted the very holiness they sought to find. It's not too late though, one can still convert the right way and undo the damage. However, it's hard for these people to admit their wrong and to come to grips with the fact that they still are not really Jewish because some misinformed rabbi has told them that they are.

This isn't some flowery book on Jewish conversion. I like to teach with complete truth and be forthcoming to my readers. When it comes to Judaism, this isn't some club to join or religious cult. Becoming Jewish is something very serious and should not be taken lightly. We don't need more sinners in Israel. Too many Jews already need reaching out to in order to return to the proper path. In fact, it is the non-Jewish seekers that have led many Jews to return back to the ways of righteousness. Many B'nei Noach have inspired Jews around the world to know G-d's Oneness and have showed them that they need to do more in order to serve Him. What B'nei Noach have done for us is priceless.

The B'nei Noach movement is flourishing throughout the world. Should one seek to awaken a new soul that is still stuck within, this book is here to embrace you and lead you on the right path. At the same time, we plan to hold nothing back so that your decision and conversion process can be one of truth and tranquility. For the B'nei Noach, this book is here to help nurture the soul and strengthen it in service of G-d. There is nothing wrong with you retaining your current status as long as you seek to observe the laws of Noah stringently and with all your heart.

CHAPTER 1:
To Know Hashem

To know Hashem (G-d), to embrace the purpose of one's existence, is to live a life of meaning and purpose. Not everyone has this. Most of the world lives their life chasing after meaningless ideas and materialism devoid of a sense of purpose.

Fear of Hashem is foundational in serving Him properly. To unconditionally love G-d, one must appreciate all the blessings of life and understand that everything that He does is for the good. It could be that your interest in converting stems from the idea of wanting to return love to Hashem. You have finally realized that there's so much to be thankful for. You seek to further embrace the One Who created you. A life of emptiness with vain pursuits no longer satisfies you. You want to embark on a journey to explore and to seek out the greatest answers. One of which is, why have I personally been created? You no longer want to live a life full of selfishness, but instead a meaningful life that returns love, appreciation and affection to your Master.

You can do this also while being a B'nei Noach. However, when it comes to rectifying the world, in order to attain the highest level of purity and spiritual growth, you will find yourself to be limited. As the years go by you can attempt to expand your knowledge and connection by delving deeper and deeper into the Torah, but your vessel cannot handle the light. To handle the light of Torah and to be a proper vessel, you must have that commitment to Judaism. This holy spark must be embraced by *halacha* observance. It should be nurtured through completing a full conversion to Judaism for without this, the upper gates of Torah will always remain closed to you.

So, where do you start in your newfound journey? This is not a simple walk in the park but is an entire change of attitude, mindset and way of life. You have to be ready to lose friendships, family and everything you've ever known. You must ask yourself, is it really worth it?

So, in order to make such a drastic change in your life you must feel G-d in everything. You must feel Him in your life to such an extent that you allow Him to fill the void of everything you will have to relinquish by becoming Jewish. You must be willing to let go of materialism, ego, idolatry, the secular lifestyle you live in, and most of the ideologies that you were raised with. Thereby only filling your life with the Devine Will of Hashem. Are you willing to give up everything for this?

To do so, you must be willing to work harder than you have ever worked, with complete connection to Hashem and His people. It is commendable of you for even considering this self-sacrifice, but I ask of you, how will you survive? Do you realize to what extent you must distance yourself from everything that you have always known? Will you be able to endure the possible financial struggles and loneliness that sometimes comes with converting?

Your new family, the Jewish people, will be great. Keep in mind though, as with all new starts, when making new friends, everything takes time and patience. It will not be easy to transform yourself into this new version of you that you wish others to embrace. That is why your connection to Hashem must be very strong. That way, all the obstacles that your new creation will face, you will persevere through them. I don't know what your expectations are but, in some ways, you should raise them and in other ways you should lower them.

About your previous difficulties in life, well some may disappear while new ones may increase. Nobody said this transformation would be easy. In fact, I am pre-warning you, telling you that it wouldn't be easy, and it will take years. There's a substantial difference between serving Hashem with seven commandments and then doing so with 613. Just like there's a difference between amateur athletes and professional ones. People expect more from the professional. Likewise, he expects even more from himself. Maybe if you're fully warned beforehand it'll be easier after you have converted.

Don't jump into Judaism with blindfolds. You must know of the hardships that the Jewish people endure. You must be aware of our suffering and that by converting, you the Newly Born Jew, will join in this suffering until the coming of the Messiah. This is nothing new. It didn't start with the Holocaust. It's been happening for thousands of years. As you see, some of our own kind have attempted to walk away from the holy Jewish way, from the path of their ancestors. This was due to the constant suffering and pressure from other nations that surround us. However, it is much harder to be content in life, pretending to be someone else, and much easier to just embrace the Jewish soul inside you.

Rabbi Menachem Mendel Schneerson writes, "The Jewish people are the heart of the world. If they are healthy, the world is healthy." (Bringing Heaven down to Earth, p. 246)

As you can see, if the world is unhealthy, it is a sign that we, the Jewish people, are unhealthy. However, G-d is following our every step and sustaining us through thick and thin. There is nowhere we walk that He isn't there guiding us and sustaining us. That is the secret of our survival. "Some [rely] upon chariots and some upon horses, but as for us, upon the Name of G-d, we call. G-d, deliver [us], the King will answer us on the day we call." (Psalms 20:8)

Is there something special about you that you see through all of our pain, a vision that its worthwhile, that there is something there for you too, nonetheless? Maybe that's why you're here seeking more spirituality.

Maybe you know something that some of us Jews don't appreciate or notice because the devotion and self-sacrifice that you will need to make this transition could be far greater than anything you have ever experienced.

May I remind you that you have a life of complete freedom only baring seven laws to govern you. We however have hundreds of responsibilities and a binding commitment to follow, some of which we don't even understand. There are many commandments that we understand and that make sense. Then there are commandments that we don't understand the deeper meaning for and won't until the redemption. Both are equally vital to our existence and service of Hashem. It's one thing to accept seven laws without understanding some of their purpose, but can you imagine hundreds like that? For example, the *mitzvah* of not wearing *shatnez* (which is a mixture of wool and linen). This Torah prohibition states that we are forbidden to wear any garment that contains both wool and linen. This is no simple thing since most labels on clothing, blankets, shoes, etc... don't list every material that was used to make the item. So, we have *shatnez* centers that even have microscopes that are used to determine if something is free of *shatnez*. We must bring items that will touch us, if there is doubt if it has *shatnez*, to be checked. There is no explanation anywhere as to why this only applies to wool and linen. Another example that is more prevalent in our lives is keeping *kosher*. Some of the laws of *kasherus* make sense. For example, the way we must slaughter the animal, is to ensure that the animal doesn't suffer. We must then inspect the animal afterwards in order to know that it was healthy and wouldn't have died of health problems, this limits the amount of illness that we can ingest from eating the animal. The laws we must keep, that are a mystery, are such as why only an animal with split hooves and that chews its cud is *kosher*. Also, the only sea animals that we can eat must have both scales and fins. These are only two examples of a larger list of *mitzvos* that we must keep without any explanation other than because Hashem said to.

Are you ready to do this? To take upon yourself countless mandatory traditions even if they cause you difficulties, sometimes making you feel uncomfortable and don't always make sense to you?

If you were to take a fish, put it on dry land, it would suffocate from the unfamiliar environment. Now if you take a person who is more complex, having lived a completely different lifestyle since they were a child, how can they be expected to adapt? Obviously, there is much more to converting than just your own personal changes, but you'll need a Higher Power to guide you. You will need Hashem above to embrace you. This will take a lot of prayer, self-searching, and patience on your part.

To know Hashem, is to do kindness to others. I believe that part of the reason you're interested in converting is because you have this kindness inside you that wants to help the world. Not everyone has this desire, and if they do it's usually for self-righteousness rather than true selflessness. The Piaseczna Rebbe stated, "The greatest thing in the world is doing another person a favor."

Rabbi Shlomo Carlebach said, "I often mention holy beggars, but people ask me who really is a holy beggar? Open your hearts my most beautiful friends. A holy beggar is someone who is begging you to allow him to give!"

"If your ears are not open to the crying of the poor, then your ears are deaf, and you will not hear G-d calling either."

The world is so full of pain, that people not only forgot how to love, they have even forgotten that true love exists. Can you imagine your children growing up in such a world? A world where some people don't even know that someone is capable of loving them?

Close your eyes and join me on a trip to Reb Shlomo Carlebach's synagogue Friday night. It's a bitter night in Manhattan and Reb Shlomo gets up to speak to the crowd.

"*Chevra* (group)!" He said.

"I have to tell you about an incident that happened to me yesterday. It troubles me so much I simply can't forget it. This is what happened: I was walking along the Upper West Side yesterday, when I saw *nebech* (sadly) a young fellow whose legs were both amputated, sitting in a wheelchair, wearing tattered clothing, begging for handouts. Everybody knows that on Broadway it's quite common to meet many unfortunate people. I approached him, gave him all the money I had, and started talking to him, 'How are you, brother? What's your name?' He gave me a strange look and didn't answer. 'So where do you live?' I continued. 'Why? What business is it of yours?' he asked suspiciously. So, I said, 'Why don't you come over to my place? I live right here on 79th street.' Again, he gave me a wary look and said, 'what do you mean?' 'I'd like to take care of you, you can stay with me; I have a synagogue over there and an apartment, too.' The man looked at me mistrustfully and said, 'No, I have gotta go!' and started pushing the wheelchair away from me.

"*Chevra*, you don't know how hard I tried. I ran after him pleading, 'You don't understand, I'm going to take care of you. I'm going to love you like you can't imagine!' He kept rolling the wheelchair away from me, and I pursued him down Broadway, until finally, I couldn't catch *mamesh* my breath anymore and I gave up."

Shlomo looked at us with anguish. "This is the most painful part of the story: the young fellow couldn't believe that I was sincere! Why do you think I am telling you what happened? To give over to you, what a terrible, tragic world we live in that this man must have been so hurt, so mislead, so abused in his lifetime, that he could no longer trust. He couldn't accept the fact that I really wanted to help him."

There is nothing more righteous than drawing closer the final redemption through kindness and *mitzvos* (commandments). The Jewish nation is a light to all the nations. Only they can truly bring perfection and sweeten the world. It's the Jewish spark that keeps the world alive and thriving. Inside the heart of every Jew is the spark that wants to inspire and bring about change. Even though some of us Jews may be lost at times, deep inside the Jewish heart is a yearning to spread truth. "My forefathers amassed riches in this world, while I have amassed souls." (Talmud Kesubos 30a) How was this done, through giving charity and helping others.

"One who acquires souls is wise." (Proverbs 11:30) By helping others, by thinking outside oneself, one acquires the next world and great wisdom.

There is an inherit thirst inside each Jewish soul that can never be fully quenched. Externally, they might show some suffering but inside they know the truth, that Hashem is One and protecting them. We go about our life knowing that there's so much more growth spiritually that we must attain. Lingering is this thirst in the soul that requires more Torah just like the physical requires food and drink.

It says in the Psalms, "I looked to the mountains, from where will my help come?" (Psalms 121:1) The Psalmist references the term "mountains". It is not just the Jewish by birth that feel as if they have a huge mountain to overcome. This is also felt by those who are looking within, trying to discover if they have a Jewish spark. A mountain stands between them to transition between gentile and Jew. The difference between the Jew overcoming this mountain is that they already have this *emes*, truth, inside them. That is their inborn holy Jewish soul. While the gentile has a yearning spark that isn't complete. This is why they are suffering so much. It is like they are trapped between two worlds. The only way they can end their suffering is to say goodbye to everything that they have known. Even being a Noahide might not be enough to quench their thirst for spiritual survival.

Just like a Jew must find the proper rabbi to help guide them, so too, must the non-Jew who is seeking conversion, find the proper rabbi for direction.

I heard the following example from my master [the Baal Shem Tov]:

"There was a road that went through the forest, passing a den of robbers, and it was very dangerous to anyone who would take it. Two people once took this road. One was insensibly drunk, while the other was sober.

"The two men were waylaid by robbers, and were robbed, beaten and wounded, barely escaping with their lives. After they reached the end of the forest, they met several people.

"Some people asked the drunk, 'Did you pass through the forest in peace?' He replied, 'It was peaceful; there is no danger at all.' They then asked him about his bruises and wounds, and he did not know how to reply. Other people raised the same question with the sober man. He replied, 'Heaven forbid! You must be very careful, for the woods are full of fierce robbers.' Speaking at great length, he warned them of the danger.

"This is the difference. A wise man knows how to warn others, so that they know not to go through the dangerous place, unless they move swiftly and are well armed. The drunkard, on the other hand does not know how to warn others at all.

"The righteous man who serves Hashem [is like the wise man]. He is fully aware of the battles waged by the Evil Urge, the robber lying on the path leading to the worship of Hashem. He is aware of the danger and is constantly alert to avoid a trap. He also knows how to warn others of the danger of the robbers. It is thus written, 'The more knowledge, the more pain.' (Ecclesiastes 1:18) The wicked man, however, [is like a drunkard]. He constantly enjoys the snares of the Evil Urge, and says, 'I am at peace-there is no danger in this world.'" (Toledos Yaakov Yosef, Ki Savo 202c)

It is important to remain focused on the end result that one must attain in order to convert. It's easy to get lost in all the Jewish literature which may not be necessary to learn yet because you enjoy the spirituality of Judaism. However, one should study that which is necessary for their conversion and not delay this by delving into many additional works. To be ready to accept their Jewish soul, they must become experts in basic *halacha*, Jewish law. One's main learning for conversion must be discussed in detail with a rabbi, and he must clarify how to prioritize your study.

In the Code of Jewish Law, it says, "He is taught some minor commandments and some major commandments, and he is taught some of the punishments for violating the commandments," but, "we do not overburden him, and we are not overly strict with him." (Shulchan Aruch, Yoreh Deah 268:2)

The logic for this is that even if the potential convert is sincere, if they are suddenly confronted with all of the stringencies, they will recoil and change their mind about converting. This is one reason why conversion isn't supposed to be sped up or rushed. It should be done slowly in order to get adapted to the new lifestyle. Nothing in Judaism, nor life, should be done to the extreme. However, this isn't an excuse to purposely delay becoming Jewish either. As we teach further in the book, if one needlessly delays keeping the *mitzvos*, just because they don't want to do them, they will have to answer for this later when they stand before the Heavenly Tribunal.

There are a few ritual requirements when one is ready to finally make the conversion official:

-The convert must undergo immersion in a Jewish ritual bath, a *mikvah*, with the appropriate prayers.

-A male convert must undergo circumcision - if they are already circumcised, a single drop of blood is drawn as a symbolic circumcision.

-One must verbally take upon themselves to observe all the 613 *mitzvos* (commandments) of the Torah.

-They have to appear before a *Beis Din* (a religious court) and obtain their approval agreeing to live a fully Jewish life.

Additionally, to these requirements, one has to be ready and already be at the level of fully keeping the *Shabbos* rituals as well as keeping *kosher*. The laws of modesty must also be kept prior to acceptance.

The Talmud (Yevamos 48) says, "A person who converts to Judaism is held responsible for his lifestyle prior to his conversion." If he did not keep the seven laws of Noah in all their particulars then he must answer for that, just as if a Jew must answer if he did not keep the 613 laws. The convert must also answer for any purposeful delay in his conversion that was unnecessary. Meaning, if they think, let me delay my conversion in order to fulfill a few more of my secular ideals, they must answer for this. The Talmud continues to explain that this is why converts suffer so much when they become Jewish.

All along, throughout their entire life, they felt their Jewish soul calling to them and awaiting to be awakened inside them. Yet they chose to ignore this. They delayed observing the Torah unnecessarily. They made excuses to put off their conversion when they knew full well that inside of them was a Jewish soul. In their very bones, they could feel the G-dliness inside them calling out. Why didn't they at least believe in the seven laws of Noah and keep them in all the particulars their entire life? These seven laws were not an option, they were the law of Heaven that had to be kept in all aspects from the day of birth.

How can this be you might ask, that one is punished for the sins prior to conversion? We learn that when a person converts it's like they're starting their entire life over? They are like a new creation. Why aren't they given a completely clean slate? Well we can compare it to the bride and groom on their wedding day. They too, are given a new slate to start over and begin anew. It is told that their sins are forgiven, and the slate is clean. It seems that it's not so simple though. One must continue to take responsibility for their actions or lack of action. Repentance is an important aspect of Judaism. It brings fear of Heaven and teaches a person to be responsible. It's true that the convert is getting new chance, but to completely eradicate our mistakes is a lifetime of doing virtuous deeds.

CHAPTER 2:
The B'nei Noach

Before considering converting to Judaism, I would strongly encourage you to adapt your lifestyle to the Noahide laws, if you haven't done so already. There are seven laws that all of mankind are commanded to follow, these are:

1. Prohibition of Idolatry
2. Prohibition of Murder
3. Prohibition of Theft
4. Prohibition of Sexual Immorality
5. Prohibition of Blasphemy
6. Prohibition of Eating Meat Taken from an Animal While it is Still Alive
7. Establishment of Courts of Law

Adopting this code would mean you can no longer pray to Jesus or Mary (if you currently do). You must truly believe in ONE G-d and place your faith solely in Him.

Once you have lived a Noahide lifestyle for an extended period it is likely you will have a better grasp in Hebrew scripture and its laws. Should you then still desire to convert to Judaism, the transition would be smoother.

The B'nei Noach movement is a very important one during these times that usher in the Messiah. It is these fine souls that will help the Jewish people by assisting our needs and they will continue in this service once the Temple is built. Their deeds will not be unnoticed, and they will be those people who will survive the preliminary wars that usher in the final Messianic times. It is known that these times have already begun and therefore, the non-Jews are running out of time to repent and to follow the commandments given to them.

If they do not accept them, they hold the burden of their souls in their hands. What will become of them? G-d's Will is that they serve Him within these laws. With all their heart and devotion, they must serve Him. If not, they will not survive the Messianic Era.

The B'nei Noach too are a light onto the nations, should they choose to be. What could be greater than to spread the Oneness of Hashem and to support His chosen people in any way possible? All of us together, doing the work of Hashem.

Some people find the seven laws to be limiting. They don't wish to become Jewish, but they want more than just these laws to guide them. Well it is told in many books that these seven actually translate into many more when it really comes down to serving Hashem.

Devoting yourself to these laws isn't a small task. For instance, the prohibition of theft branches out into many aspects of your life. We think of stealing as actually removing an item that doesn't belong to us and taking possession of it. Here are some other practical examples of its observance.

If someone is sleeping, especially one's parents, awakening them without a good reason is like stealing their sleep. Throughout the rest of the day, they might be tired and not function to their full capacity.

When it comes to business, one should always give the customer an honest purchase. Not overcharging them or selling them an item that is not the very best for them. There is so much dishonesty in business today.

If you have a boss, but while are paying you to work an hourly wage, you take time away from working in order to check your social media, this is stealing. I could go on and on about just this one law, but I think I made my point.

Let's quickly take the prohibition of murder. If someone approaches you who is poor, doesn't have food and you don't provide them their basic needs, this could be a form

34

of murder if it puts their life in harm's way. As we were saying with the previous law, it's very important to do business without hurting another person. Should you take more than is correct from a poor customer it is stealing. The Talmud says that a poor person is similar to a dead person. If they have no money, they feel as if they are nothing and that life doesn't feel worth living.

Now let's brush upon the prohibition of idolatry. If a person doesn't have faith in G-d, if they truly don't believe that all things and occurrences come from Him, this lack of faith is a form of idolatry.

If you are stubborn and self-centered, this too is a form of idolatry as it's like you worship yourself instead of the Creator. Should you be too involved in politics, thinking that these people really control every aspect of your life, this is a lack of faith.

So, as I was saying, the responsibility of being a B'nei Noach is nothing to frown upon. It is huge and a great deed to observe these seven holy laws. Should you truly wish to still become Jewish after perfecting them, who are we to stop you? Just know, you don't have to feel any pressure making that next step unless you're sure of yourself. Listen deeply to your heart and pray a lot. Let Hashem guide you and lead you on the path of truth.

The Baal Shem Tov taught: It is written [that Hashem told Avraham], "Look to the heavens and count the stars... so will be your children." (Bereshis 15:5)

The stars appear very small, but in heaven they are really very large. The same is true of Israel. Down in this [physical] world, they appear very small, but in the world on high, they are really very large. (Rabbi Tzvi Hirsh of Zidichov, Beis Yisrael, Lech Lecha; Quoted in Sefer Baal Shem Tov, Lech Lecha 27)

Don't take for granted anyone who is Jewish. I think some B'nei Noach can trick themselves into thinking they can reach as high or similar to the Jewish soul. Just like the *Levi* must understand that his place is under the *Kohein* in the

Temple. He respects that his job too is important for the greater good and special.

It is written, "Hashem said to Moshe: 'Come up to Me to the mountain… and I will give you the tablets of stone, the Torah and the commandments…'" (Exodus 24:12) Our sages interpret this to teach us that everything was given to Moshe on Sinai. (Berachos 5a)

Every discipline, whether it be geometry, mathematics, or any of the "seven branches of wisdom", is alluded to in the Talmud. One of the listeners questioned this, maintaining that there are many people who know the Talmud very well, yet have no idea of these other disciplines.

Let me tell you a parable that will better explain this. Once there was a king who had many treasures, one greater than the next. He had one son and many servants.

When the king became old, he realized that he would have to hide his treasures very cleverly if they were not to be stolen by his servants after his death. He acted wisely and hid all his important treasures in various buildings, as well as in the walls of the palace and in his own private chambers.

The places where these treasures were hidden were marked only with a slight differentiation in the pattern of the wall, so that only a very cleaver individual would be able to find the place. The more important the treasure, the more it was hidden, and the subtler the differentiation.

After the king had completed all this, he took his son aside, and told him privately, "Know that everything that I am doing is in vain. Pay close attention and you will understand."

When the king died, all his treasures that were hidden in obvious places were grabbed up by his servants. Heeding his father's words, the son scrutinized the walls very carefully until he found a slight difference. He then broke down the wall and found an important treasure. He then looked even more carefully, and found more subtle differentiations, indicating even more valuable treasures.

The parallel is that the other forms of wisdom were grabbed up by the servants, who are the nations of the world.

The important treasures are those that include the fear of Hashem, and these are hidden away for the only son. The treasury that is the most important of all is the one that includes "burning love". (Shir Hashirim 3:10, cf Metzudos ad loc.) (Toldos Yaakov Yosef, BeHar 123d)

The Baal Shem Tov taught, "A person comes into a store where they sell many types of delicacies and sweetmeats. The first thing the storekeeper does is to give him a sample of each kind, in order that the customer should have an idea of what to buy. When he tastes it and sees how good it is, he wants to sample more. The storekeeper then says, "You have to pay for anything you take. We do not give away anything free here."

The "free sample" is the light that a person feels when they first begin to draw close [to Hashem]. Through the taste of this light, they can subjugate all evil, and return everything to the ultimate good. This is [a "free sample"] given to the individual so that they should know the taste of serving Hashem. A mark (reshimu) of this remains after [this light] is withdrawn, in order that they should know what to seek. (Rabbi Yitzchok Isaac of Kamarna, Otzer HaChaim, Nasso 3c, quoted in Sefer Baal Shem Tov, Noah 14)

Similarly, the B'nei Noach is given a small taste of Judaism. If they want to have it, they have to work very hard to be worthy of the treasure. They have already become more blessed than the rest of the world with a small taste of the commandments. Should they want them all, they don't come without a price. If one only wants to acquire knowledge, they will not merit to perceive anything. Regarding them it is written, "All flesh is like grass, and all of its kindness is like the flower of the field." (Yeshayahu 40:6)

However, if one longs to cleave to Hashem and to become a vehicle (Merkavah) for Him, the only way to do so is through the Torah and mitzvos. Then, whether one engages in the revealed teachings or the hidden teachings, they will be a Merkavah for Hashem. (Keter Shem Tov 174)

Just like a Jewish soul is a servant of G-d, so too are B'nei Noach. Knowing that people recognize them to be different, they too have a responsibility to make a *kiddush* Hashem, sanctify G-d's Name. Therefore, they must work very hard on character correction. The people they are around should notice a difference in their behavior from others. They are after-all a special people with higher standards.

The Baal Shem Tov says, "When a person speaks a word of good, that word is his life force, but life force comes from Hashem, and therefore, that word rises on high and awakens the Supernal World. This causes more life force to be transmitted to the individual from on high.

"When a person speaks evil, however, then he spews forth his life force, but it does not ascend on high. It is thus possible for him to lose all his life force. People therefore say that 'He spoke out (*Er hat ois ge-ret*).'" (Tzava'as HaRivash 102)

Repentance is fundamental to the lives of someone trying to serve Hashem. There will be many ups and downs, but you still must do everything in your power to stand uprightly before Hashem. Therefore, after sinning, you too must search for light in the darkness of your sin. You too, must feel rattled by your lack of serving G-d. There is enough holiness in your seven commandments to lead you on a just path.

The Baal Shem Tov continues, "When a person brings a candle into a dark place, the darkness disappears completely and is no longer visible. The same is true when a person repents. Even though he was previously in a place of darkness, when it is illuminated with the light of the Torah, the darkness disappears completely." (Degel Machaneh Ephraim, Likkutim 84b, quoted in Sefer Baal Shem Tov, Netzavim 4)

We are taught that in the case of [Elisha ben Abuyah, otherwise known as Acher (the other,)] a heavenly voice proclaimed, "Return, return, children who would return, except for Acher." (Chagigah 15a)

The Baal Shem Tov taught that it was Acher's punishment that he should be cast aside. But still, if he had pressed forward and returned, he would have been accepted. There is nothing that can stand up before repentance.

(Yerushalmi Peah 5a; Yerushalmi, Sanhedrin 49a; Zohar 2:106a) (Shevachei HaBaal Shem Tov p. 50)

The Talmud teaches that, "In the place where those who have repented stand, even the perfectly righteous cannot stand." (Berachos 34b) What does this mean exactly as I know I am so far from the place of the *tzaddikim*?

The Baal Shem Tov also addresses this question. He says, "I heard a reason why the person who repents is greater. He already knows the heat and enthusiasm of sin. Therefore, when he repents and becomes involved in Torah and virtuous deeds, he does everything with great enthusiasm and intensity. He knows the meaning of enthusiasm, which is not true of the righteous person who has never experienced it."

Charitable deeds and Torah study can become habitual for a righteous person, and he does not have that much feeling for them. But when a person comes back, everything is new. If he does not do everything with great attachment, he will fall from his level. He is therefore forced to worship with great enthusiasm. (Or Torah, Toledos, quoted in Sefer Baal Shem Tov, Netzavim 6)

The enthusiasm that I have seen from B'nei Noach is mindboggling. I'm very impressed. In a certain way, it might be easier for the future convert to serve Hashem, since their soul has a hidden Jewish soul inside it, but for the B'nei Noach to find Hashem, is truly remarkable in our generation.

The greatness of the Holy One, blessed be He, is primarily revealed when the non-Jewish nations, too, come to know that there is a Divine Authority. As the Zohar states: "When the idolatrous priest Jethro decided to serve G-d and declared, 'Now I know that G-d is greater than all powers,' the Divine name was glorified and exalted from every aspect." (Zohar II, Yisro, 69a, citing Exodus 18:11) (Rabbi Nachman of Breslov, Likutei Moharan I, 10:1)

"And Jethro the Priest of Midian, father-in-law of Moses, heard of all that G-d had done for Moses and for Israel, His people…" (Exodus 18:1). Because he was the father-in-law of Moses, he heard and converted. For everything Moses worked to accomplish, during his life and now, after his death, was only to make converts [and bring all humanity back to G-d] (Rabbi Nachman of Breslov, Likutei Moharan 1:215).

Through converts (*gerim*) and Jews who have returned to Torah Judaism (*ba'alei teshuvah*), the Oneness of G-d is revealed through the very multiplicity of creation. Since they, too, come forth in order to become incorporated into His absolute Oneness, this is most precious to G-d. Therefore, the Torah stresses that one should love and encourage the proselyte. Similarly, our sages greatly praised the spiritual levels attained by penitents, who, after having distanced themselves, strive to return to G-d. (Rabbi Noson Sternhartz, Likutei Halachos, Prika Ute'ina, 4:3)

"Peace, peace, to the far and the near." (Isaiah 57:19) Converts and *ba'alei teshuvah* often feel the pain of their distance from holiness, due to their past sins and the extent to which they have not yet purified their bodies. Nevertheless, they must also realize how close they truly are to G-d - just as they are right now - for G-d's love and mercy is limitless. When they grasp this, they can draw close to Him. These two seemingly opposite perceptions are implied by the verse, "Peace, peace to the far and the near."

This principle is also reflected by the tradition that when a non-Jew comes to convert, he is initially discouraged (Yevamos 47a). This is a consequence of his distance from holiness. However, the entire purpose of this initial discouragement is only to strengthen his resolve and draw him closer. For if after everything, he says, "I know that I am unworthy," that is, he recognizes his distance from holiness, then he is immediately accepted. (Rabbi Noson Sternhartz, Likutei Halachos, Shilu'ach HaKan 5:17)

In the Ultimate Future, speech will be perfected. Even the non-Jewish nations will use their power of speech to call out to G-d, as it is written, "For then I will convert the nations to a pure speech, that they shall all call upon the name of G-d." (Zephaniah 3:9) Thus, speech will be perfected.

At present, speech is lacking and incomplete, for the

entire world is not using the power of speech to call out to G-d. However, in the ultimate future, they will all use the power of speech to call out to G-d, even the non-Jewish nations. Then speech will be perfected. This is the aspect of "a pure speech," since everyone will use speech to call out to G-d. (Rabbi Nachman of Breslov, Likutei Moharan I, 66:3)

I really believe that the main power in the B'nei Noach is his words.

The Baal Shem Tov says, "That Hashem is present in every movement. It is impossible to make any move or speak any word without His power." (Keter Shem Tov 273)

It is the words of a person that separate him from human verses animal form. No creature except a human can speak. When the B'nei Noach speaks words of praise to Hashem, he elevates himself and those around him.

He doesn't have the *mitzvah* of eating *kosher* or *Shabbos* or even circumcision. These things are what makes a Jew different and he is lacking them. However, for the B'nei Noach, it is his speech that sets him apart. A person becomes holy through one of two ways, his speech or his guarding of sexual purity. If you think about it, speech is the gift given to the B'nei Noach. It is what differentiates him from other nations, in my opinion.

Brad talks about his search for G-d. He grew in Texas from a Southern Baptist upbringing. He began to question his base in Christianity around the age of 12. Over the years he abandoned all aspects of organized religion, feeling a spiritual void, he began to study the various religions of the world. Through this study he came to develop his own philosophy, his definition of G-d. With this, he began to establish what his relationship with G-d was to be. He found that the product of his search was what Judaism is. Brad describes his process to conversion as, "wandering in the desert for many years before determining that (his) beliefs coincided with those of Judaism." He undertook formal conversion at the remarkable age 51. I guess you can say from Brad's story, "that it is never too late to convert."

I think it's important not to overlook how during Brads struggle to find himself, he relied heavily on speech. Not just regular talking to others but personally connecting to Hashem in the form of *hisbodidus*, Jewish meditation.

Steven writes me, "When I'm all alone with Hashem in *hisbodidus* it's as if time itself stands still and I can see clearly again. As one who has pondered the cost of conversion for quite some time, I often need my mind and time to stand still and for my soul to be calmed by the Creator's words. With so many questions and much self-reflection, one can feel as if they are overwhelmed and in despair especially living outside of a Jewish community. However, from my honest observation it's as if the Creator speaks to you no matter who you are (Jew or non-Jew) even if you have committed sins that trouble your soul and give you restless nights. Hashem will not give up on you as His great love for you outweighs everything else. He has invested a part of Himself in the soul of every human being. Wise men, even rabbis, can give you advice and great answers to big questions but only Hashem can solve and calm the inward turmoil of one's soul. What is true prayer and devotion but a lifelong wrestle against your lower sensual self in order to come higher and be all that Hashem has created you to be."

For Steven, *hisbodidus* is necessary for his survival as a searching B'nei Noach, without it, he would be completely lost. *Hisbodidus* is therefore fundamental for Steven and others like him.

You can take the greatest Jewish sinner and still find within them a special light of kindness. The Jews had trouble hiding from the Nazi's not just because they looked Jewish, they couldn't hide their finer character traits. Even if they tried, it was almost impossible to completely blend into the goyish world. A Jew, no matter what, still has a special spark inside them.

We learn in the book, Sha'ar HaGilgulim that in our day and age, most souls that come down are reincarnations. There are few new souls being created. Some of these souls are so holy, that the Satan fights to keep these souls from coming back into the world. When he eventually loses, since they are still destined to arrive and complete themselves, he debates until the soul is given to families that are far from Hashem. This soul must then find a way back.

While the soul might be too holy to enter a non-Jewish body, I wonder if its spark could possibly enter a non-Jew, but this could only happen with much prayer to G-d and through the sages of the generation.

So, I wonder, if a B'nei Noach wanted more from their life, could they pray their way into a Jewish soul? Prayer is very powerful, but still the non-Jew is not above the *mazalos* (celestial bodies that effect one's life) to change their destiny so easily. However, with much prayer and coming to the *tzaddik*, sage, this could possibly change. After all, the sage has been given the keys to uphold G-d's world. This is no simple task and would take a tremendous self-nullification to accomplish. When I ran this concept by someone, they commented that if their yearning is so strong to begin with, most probably they truly have a Jewish soul to uncover.

You know everything can be nullified in G-d's light. That is how we, the Jewish people are so holy. Through our humility, we gain closeness. When you reach elevated levels of humility, anything can happen. You become connected to the concepts of miracles and the inner point of creation itself.

Even though in general, we are forbidden to convert someone just because they love their Jewish boyfriend or girlfriend, we might be very slightly more open-minded about it. This is because we don't want to lose the Jewish soul that might leave his religion for love. However, converting someone only for this reason is shunned upon for good reason. A convert must become Jewish because of their great love for the *mitzvos*. They must feel a Jewish soul awakening inside them, but I wonder, which is why we might be open to hear their case at rare intervals, if this connecting to their Jewish partner is their soul's recognition of the greatness of Judaism. Maybe they needed to meet this person in order to awaken the Jewish soul they already have, but still, we don't convert someone over love. They have to be completely committed.

If you're a B'nei Noach, or someone on the path of conversion, please avoid being in such a situation to begin with. I have seen to many converts already looking to date before they complete their conversion. Your conversion must come first. Take yourself off the market.

Also, if you're Jewish and hanging around with the opposite sex often because of school or business, make a separation. Don't allow yourself to fall for someone who hasn't decided to convert on their own. Avoid these situations to begin with. I have also noticed some B'nei Noach women being overly friendly with single Jewish men. I've had to call out to some of them, both sides, to make some distance. Please as a B'nei Noach, respect the modesty we are commanded to keep as Jews and vice versa.

Steven asks me, "What do you do when you want to remain a B'nei Noach and your wife is ahead spiritually, ready to convert?" I suggested that she slows down a bit in order for him to catch up and convert together, even if it will add a few years to the transformation. Though it's important, it is still not a rush to convert, and it's much easier as a family to do it together. Conversion, anyway, is a process that takes years of study.

However, you will find that the calling might be too great to dismiss. Sometimes it takes one spouse to pull the other up. This often takes place inside *ba'alei teshuva* families, that one of the spouses is pushing far ahead of the other. I've seen the good and bad of such situations. It really can cause a lot of friction. However, if you truly love someone, you will go down to where they are and be there with them. Even if you slowly have to go to the pits of hell and back, you feel responsible to make them happy and save them. So sometimes, you have to get a little bit dirty in the process and that too might be justified at times.

Rebbe Nachman has a cute story about a boy who thought he was a turkey. The boy would hide under the table and act strangely. The father, seeing that the only way to raise his child up from this behavior, descended with the child under the table acting similarly to him. After a while, they both were able to rise together from this place.

The Talmud says about the world to come that a wife can bring her husband up, but he can't bring her down from her reward. I think in most cases, women being more spiritual beings, will seek to find their way closer to G-d first. A lot also depends on a person's personality. People that think and reflect a lot, seem to search more for answers. Someone that is more fun by nature, not as deep, may not desire so much change in his life. He is happy with the status quo. Thank G-d, I was born Jewish, but if I weren't, I would be very overwhelmed by the conversion process. I certainly wouldn't rush it, not because I wouldn't want to convert but because change is difficult for me. Each day for breakfast, I eat the same salmon meal with a fresh glass of water. When I walk or travel, I use the same route. Your spouse might be the opposite. For them, change is something they embrace. They love traveling and new adventures.

It doesn't warrant converting a spouse just because you wish to stay married. You both have to be ready and feel like conversion is right for each of you individually. The Torah is very big on families staying together. It says that the *Shechinah*, Devine Presence, cries over broken families. If you're married, you need to each take a step back and do what is right as individuals and also as a family.

Even though you may be ready to convert, it doesn't mean your children are ready to handle this major change. It is so much better to convert when the child is very young, that way they can grow up feeling Jewish. Converting when older, seems to really be taxing on children. Often the parents are baiting them to follow *halachos*, Jewish laws, when they just want to be like their *goyish* friends. This situation is very tricky, and it is important that you are wise, so that the children's desire to become Jewish is their own, and it isn't about your pushing them. They must feel comfortable and make the decision themselves. It takes a lot of patience and also some

45

separation from non-Jews who will discourage them with a lot
of negativity. Surround them with light and hopefully this will
rub off on them. Maybe homeschooling them would be a first
place to start, but this too has its challenges. One thing we learn
with raising our kids, everything is about showing your passion
for the *mitzvos*. Children and people in general thrive off of
witnessing people performing the *mitzvos* with all their heart. It
is important to understand that in the end they might not
choose to become Jewish. This is a reality you must be ready
to accept.

I was once approached by a holy Jew that was engaged
to be married to a non-Jew. He could not imagine himself
changing his whole life and ending the relationship, just to
return to the Torah way. However, I encouraged him daily, and
we became close friends. I promised him that if he leaves her,
G-d will send him his rightful, Jewish match right away. Indeed,
three months later, *mazal tov*, he was engaged to an Israeli girl.
His relationship with his family strengthened once again as
they had previously distanced themselves from him. However,
when he returned to keeping *Shabbos* and the *mitzvos*, they
reunited happily.

However, the Israeli girl was not yet on the level of
keeping the commandments. I suggested to him to be patient
with her and go up in religious growth together. Generally
speaking, I advise people to look for a match that suits them
on their level of Judaism. This really should be fundamental
when looking for your *bashert* (soul mate), but G-d is full of
surprises.

I once had a Jewish friend that fell in love with a girl
before she finished her conversion. He even moved to the
same town and moved in with her. What a horrible thing to
have happened, not only did he become less religious, she
never converted in the end and found someone else. The
situation destroyed this lonely Jew looking for companionship.
He thought he was going to help her convert but, in the end,
she converted him away from Hashem. This again poses the
question, why were they so close to begin with? It wasn't a

modest friendship according to the Torah. They both should not have been talking to one another.

B'nei Noach have always struggled finding partners. Years ago, I tried to fix this through creating a social media platform that I advertised very well. However, I think this fix has to come from the B'nei Noach themselves. I found few really willing to sacrifice it all to help out with their own movement. Overtime, I noticed that the problem wasn't rabbis like myself who might have been ignoring them. It was rather because of their confusion in thinking that they might decide to become Jewish one day that they hadn't wholeheartedly devoted themselves to the movement itself.

This somewhat brings me back to the question I have today, are most B'nei Noach simply converts in transition? Do they feel comfortable and satiated remaining a B'nei Noach?

Now I can't make that decision for you. You have to decide it for yourselves, but throughout the rest of the book, I'm going to assume that my assumption is true, you're seeking more, and you think one day you might convert. Therefore, I am going to show you the truth of Judaism and its beauty. Thereafter, you decide with much heart-searching, what is the right path for you.

I think the biggest struggle for both the convert and B'nei Noach is depression and loneliness. This comes from the holiness of these two pathways and the isolation it can bring. With both, you don't generally have physical people around you that understand you and support your motives. You feel somewhat abandoned, unloved and on your own. Your inner voice has become silent as there aren't many who understand you. However, G-d seems to keep calling and you only wish you could answer, being the best servant, you can be.

In an attempt to console one of these searchers, I wrote to them, "Awesome self-searching and the main thing is to stay happy. Within the pain and confusions, Hashem is there with you. There is no reason to be sad." I think you have to be confident and proud of yourself that you have come so far. There is no reason to despair.

The Baal Shem Tov writes, "You should always know everything in the world is filled with Hashem, as it is written, 'Do I not fill heaven and earth?' (Jeremiah 23:24)

"Everything that is created through the power of man's thoughts or plans is all from Hashem. Even the most trivial things in the world are all the results of Hashem's providence.

"When you realize this, you will know that when you want to do something, it does not make any difference whether it comes out the way you desired. Everything comes from Hashem, and He knows that it is best for you when some things do not come out as you desire.

"You should therefore never be annoyed or distressed when you want to do something and are not successful. You know that this is Hashem's will. If Hashem had thought it right, He would certainly have helped you achieve success. Your very lack of success is therefore an indication that it was not Hashem's will for you do this thing. Hashem therefore did you a favor and did not allow you a success [that might have been harmful to you]." (Hanhagos Yesharos 10a, quoted in Sefer Baal Shem Tov, Miketz 11)

You don't know how wonderful it is that you have separated yourself from the other nations. The western civilizations don't seem to get it. They keep on thinking that love and compassion towards all false religions will bring peace and truth. Philosophies that were created on the basis of idol worship or false prophets are built from lies and deceit. Interestingly whatever little "truths" or "wisdom" they may appear to have were stolen from the Torah and Talmud.

It's hard not to notice as a gentile that there is something special about the Jewish people. If the B'nei Noach were to physically be around Jews for most of his day, it could be he would feel the pull needed to convert. We see this from the following example.

Rabbi Elimelech teaches: "The Talmud says, 'Israel was exiled only in order that they should receive proselytes.' (Pesachim 87b)

"At first, this is difficult to understand. Is it fitting that

Israel should be exiled in order to accept converts? It would seem more appropriate that the nations should come to the Land of Israel by themselves and be converted there.

"The concept, however, is this. The thing that motivates a gentile to become a proselyte is the holy spark that is in him. The spark is very weak, however, and it does not have the power to lift his heart and bring him to the land of Israel to convert of his own accord. But when he sees the Jews and gazes upon them [since they are exiled among the goyim], the holiness of Israel gives strength, power and motivation to that holy spark in him, and this motivates him to become a proselyte. It is for this reason that Israel had to be exiled." (Noam Elimelech, Yisro 41a)

In another instance, the rebbe comments more on this concept. He asks, why should Israel have to undergo the suffering of exile for this purpose? Would it not have been better if G-d had brought the nations to the land of Israel so that they could be proselytized there?

When a righteous person wants to accomplish something, he must first lower himself from his usual level. Only then can he accomplish [anything with those on a lower level]. This is because each thing can only be acted upon by that which resembles and parallels it.

It is known that the holiness of the land of Israel is very great. It was therefore impossible for Israel to accomplish the ingathering of proselytes there. When the Jews are in the land of Israel, their holiness is very great, and they are totally separated from all nations. They, therefore, have no relationship to them and cannot parallel them and break the power [of evil] in them, allowing them to become proselytes.

It was for this reason that Israel was exiled. When they are outside their land, their holiness is reduced, and they can attract proselytes. Even though a righteous man may be on an elevated level of holiness, he can lower himself somewhat, and to some extent, identify with the gentile who comes to convert.

The holiness of the land of Israel, however, is so great that even if the righteous man were to lower himself somewhat, he would still be on a high plane of holiness. Therefore, as long as he is in the land, he cannot in any way identify with the essence of the gentile who comes to convert. (Noam Elimelech, Likutei Shoshanah 98b)

To summarize, there is a huge responsibility for the Jew to elevate sparks. The entire creation is based on this concept. The sparks of creation fell to all places and it takes a lot of *mitzvos* and good deeds to elevate them. That is why 613 commandments were needed. Seven commandments also allow for some elevation of sparks.

It is strange though, if the religious man is to stay away from evil, you would think that he would stay far away from the other nations. Anyway, we see that he is brought down to these low places. No wonder so much of the Jewish population became assimilated and lost. They were dispersed to be among those who do not believe in G-d or worship idolatry.

So, what do the wise do, they isolate themselves and frequent Jewish places and holy places, staying away from non-Jewish influences which may harm their soul. However, that seems to defeat the purpose of their exile which is to be thrown into the mix.

You know if you put someone amidst dirty water, eventually, they too will get wet with filth. Therefore, it's not that the Jew must assimilate and make friends with the non-Jew in order to return them and the light. The potential convert and B'nei Noach only need to encounter the Jewish light from afar, be slightly in its presence and that will be enough to light their spark of return.

Do you know how many B'nei Noach or converts never said a word to a Jew yet admired them from afar? Quite a lot. So, it's the job of the Jew not to assimilate more than necessary but to be enough of a light to inspire. Those who are meant to return or convert, will thereby know what to do for themselves. That is why we don't actually have to go out and make converts. We allow them to come find us through setting a good example.

Here is an interesting parable that might explain this. A

musician was once playing a most beautiful melody, with a wonderous rhythm and all the sweetness in the world. All those who heard him were captured by the sweetness and joy of his melody, and they danced until they almost touched the ceiling.

The entire room was thus filled with boundless joy, rhythm and sweetness. The closer one came to the musician, the closer he would bring himself, having even more pleasure and dancing all the more.

In the middle of all this, a deaf man came along who could not hear the beautiful music at all. All he saw were people wildly dancing, and he thought that they were mad. His only remark was, "What kind of joy is this?"

If this deaf man was wise, he would have understood that something was motivating the people, and he would have known that a very beautiful melody was being played. If he had understood this, he too would have danced with them. The parallel is obvious. (Degel Machanah Ephraim, Yisro 35a)

Sometimes I hear so many excuses from people as to why they can't take upon themselves the next level to convert to Judaism. Here is an interesting parable from Rebbe Nachman just to get you thinking.

A great general girded himself for battle and had to overcome a mighty wall. When he came to the gate, he found it blocked with a spider web.

Could you imagine anything more foolish than returning in defeat because a spider web is blocking your path? (Sichos Haran 232)

You might wonder why once you find G-d, things feel more difficult and even more confusing. Rebbe Nachman has some interesting words about this. He says, "When a person begins... truly to serve G-d, he is often beset by evil thoughts and confusions.

Actually, the evil was always there, but it is only now surfacing. A pot of water may seem to be perfectly clear, but when it is placed on a fire and begins to boil, all its impurities are brought to the surface. One must stand by and constantly remove these impurities.

The original purity is merely an illusion. With a little heat the impurity surfaces, but when these impurities are removed, the water is truly pure and clear.

The same is true of a person. Before he begins serving G-d, good and evil are completely mixed together within him. The impurities are so closely united with the good that they cannot be recognized.

When this person comes close to a true *tzaddik* they begin to burn with great feeling toward G-d. He is touched with the heat of purification, and all the evil and impurities come to the surface. Here again one must stand by and constantly remove the dirt and impurities as they appear. In the end the person is truly pure and clear.

Purification requires this period of agitation and confusion. In the beginning a person is totally immersed in the material. He then begins to come close to G-d.

It would seem possible to remove this dirt and impurity at once, but his mind is completely intermingled with this mire. Were it to be removed immediately, his mind would be drawn out with it.

Therefore, one must be purified little by little, in gradual stages. (Sichos Haran 79)

I think it's really important to take a step back and really appreciate how far you have come already. To give thanks to Hashem for raising you above the confusions of other religions and to have found Him. This itself is very great and you should be proud of yourself for arriving at this point.

It is written, "Only good and love with pursue me all the days of my life." (Psalms 23:6) The Baal Shem Tov explains that very often a person does not know what is good for him. What man is so wise as to understand what is best for him? Good may pursue him as a result of G-d's love, since He wants to reveal a light of hope and prosperity to this individual. But he turns his back on it and runs away from the things that are truly good for him. He does not realize that if he only accepted them, he would profit and be successful.

This was King David's prayer for all Israel: "Only good

and love should pursue me. You want to grant me good and love, but I do not have the sense to accept it, and I may still be running away from it. I therefore pray that it should pursue me to such an extent that I am not able to run away from it. Let it pursue me until I accept it and bring it home." (Likutey Torah Mahari, Ki Savo)

I wonder if for some people, the heavenly signs that they should pursue conversion have been hovering over them for years, yet they are still waiting. They are waiting for some angel to drop from heaven, teach them all the laws of *Shabbos* and keeping *kosher*, immerse them in the *mikvah*, all while they are sleeping. The obvious signs don't seem to be enough. Maybe they want G-d to hand deliver a letter to them saying, "Dear creation of mine, I want you to be Jewish so start immediately to take classes." Do you really think your worthy of such a sign? Hasn't He already done enough to show you the proper path?

In the case of Amalek, they would not submit to G-d even when they saw His miracles and wonders. When you realize how blessed you are and that everything around you is a miracle, it starts to transition your mindset.

The Maggid of Mezrich taught, "Nothing can change from one thing to another [without first losing its original identity]. Thus, for example, before an egg can grow into a chicken, it must completely cease to be an egg. Each thing must lose its original identity before it can be something else.

Therefore, before a thing is transformed into something else, it must come to the level of nothingness. This is how a miracle comes about, changing the laws of nature. First the thing must be elevated to the Emanation of Nothingness. Influence then comes from that Emanation to produce the miracle." (Maggid Devarav LeYaakov 54)

This is what happens as someone grows into a convert. He is leaving the shell and takes upon himself a new identity. The B'nei Noach is a bit different. He always had the seven laws to follow, he just didn't know about them nor fully understand them. So really, even though he changes, it's not like he is taking upon himself a completely new life form as if he were converting. Still though, through both of these changes, there has to be a level of nothingness reached in order to make that plunge into new waters. G-d is infinite, and no vessel can hold Him at all, except when a person makes them self like nothing. Only when the non-Jew has reached the level of total humility, can they then become Jewish. Then they literally become transformed.

You cannot reach this level if you attach yourself to physical, worldly things. You must relinquish your desire for materialism foremost. Your troubles and worries, you must forget them along with your ego. This is the path towards finding G-d.

CHAPTER 3:
Having Faith

Whether you're a gentile or Jew, everyone needs to strengthen their faith in Hashem. Rebbe Nachman says that faith is the foundation of believing and serving G-d. Even simply speaking to others about faith will help to increase your own faith.

The Rebbe once encouraged a person who was greatly confused about his beliefs. Rebbe Nachman told him, "It is written that all creation was brought into being only because of people like you. G-d saw that there would be people who would cling to our holy faith, suffering greatly because of the confusion and doubts that constantly would plague them. He perceived that they would overcome these doubts and remain strong in their beliefs. It was because of this that G-d brought forth all of creation."

This individual was greatly strengthened and was subsequently unperturbed when he had these confusing thoughts.

On numerous other occasions, Rebbe Nachman said that the creation was mainly for the sake of faith. It is thus written, "All His works are through faith." (Psalms 33:4) (Sichos Haran 222)

Even for the great rabbis who were known for the wonderous wisdom, to them, their faith was kept simple. Rabbi Chaim of Tzanz would often pace back and forth in a room, totally absorbed in his holy thoughts and meditations. All the while, he was immersed in loving awareness of the L-rd his G-d, blessed be He. From time to time he would cry out, "There is no place where He is not!" Other times, he would call out,

"He fills all worlds and surrounds all worlds!" Sometimes he would call out the Thirteen Articles of Faith. (My Book, Pathways of the Righteous p. 20)

Many times, Rabbi Nachman said that no sophistication is needed in serving G-d. All that is required is simplicity, sincerity, and faith. Rabbi Nachman said that simplicity is the highest possible level. G-d is certainly higher than all else, but G-d is ultimately simple. (Sichos Haran 101)

All too often people complicate their service of G-d. Faith being the foundation of all service, is ultimately a simple concept. All the philosophers try to scientifically prove everything. They ask question upon questions making belief simply impossible. They are wise in doing this as it makes everyone so confused that it makes them look wise. However, faith is simple without any confusion, it is just faith. That there is One G-d in heaven and on earth that runs everything according to His Will.

When the Nazis invaded Austria, Shlomo's father Rabbi Naftali Carlebach, called a family conclave to discuss a plan of action. Soon, all the family members were assembled in the dining room, everyone that is but eleven-year-old Shlomo. Repeated calls for the missing twin elicited no response, and Shlomo's mother, Rebbetzin Paula Carlebach, was dispatched by her husband to search for him throughout the family's spacious quarters.

A few minutes later, she turned breathless, her eyes wild with fear. "Shlomo's nowhere to be found," she replied in tense, clipped tones. "I've looked for him everywhere. He's definitely not in the apartment. Oh, my G-d," the Rebbetzin clutched her heart in consternation, "he must have gone outside."

Shlomo had been repeatedly warned by his parents that it was no longer safe to venture outdoors. He was a boy of unusual courage and determination, but he was also a respectful and obedient child, who almost always honored this parents' wishes. Could he have flagrantly flouted their authority this time? And for what purpose? Why would he have left the relative safety of their home? Where could he have gone?

Rabbi Carlebach instructed the family to disperse and check all the rooms a second time. Once again, they returned emptyhanded. Shlomo had not been found, and panic was beginning to set in.

Suddenly, Shlomo's twin, Eli Chaim, had an inspiration. "I know where he is," he shouted triumphantly. "Follow me!"

"So Shloimala," said Rabbi Carlebach softly, as he ascended to the top of the house and spied his eleven-year-old son from a distance, "what are you doing on the roof?"

"*Tatta*! (father)" Shlomo turned to Rabbi Carlebach with burning eyes, "the roof is that much closer to Hashem (G-d). "And at a time like this, shouldn't we try to be as close to G-d as much as possible?"

Rebbe Menachem Mendel Schneerson writes, "Life is a game of hide and seek. G-d hides, we seek.

"Everywhere in the world, parents play peek-a-boo with their children. It is a major discovery of life, a cornerstone in human development: To realize that something is there even when you cannot see it, that the world is not defined by your subjective perception, that there is something that absolutely is-whether you know of it or not.

"All our life, all of the world, is G-d playing with us that same game. He peeks with a miracle and then hides behind nature. Eventually, we look behind nature to find Him there." (Bringing Heaven down to Earth, p. 45)

There are two ways to look at nature and science. You can look upon it and recognize the oneness and power of G-d, or you can see it only from the standpoint of natural causes. My wise seven-year-old once commented, "Hashem is a painter and we are in His painting."

The Koznitzer Maggid writes, "The heresy of the Egyptians and [other idolaters] who followed the children of Israel out of Egypt was as follows; they admitted G-d's greatness, and realized that He is Infinite, and that no thought can encompass Him at all. They also knew that we cannot speak of will or any other attribute with regard to G-d's essence.

"This being so, [they asked,] how can we say that G-d deals with man according to his deeds, or that He desires that we keep the Torah and its commandments? How can we say that G-d has any enjoyment or pleasure from those who keep His commandments? Would this not be a deficiency for an Infinite Being?

"These people therefore denied G-d's providence over the physical world. According to their understanding, this would not be proper according to His greatness and glory.

"They then went further with their heresy and called, 'the G-d of gods.'" (Succah 29a)

People ask many questions regarding G-d. [Rabbi Nachman] often said that it is only fitting that there be many difficulties in our understanding of G-d. This is correct and proper according to His greatness and lofty nature.

G-d is so exceedingly great and high that He is far above our minds. It is therefore inevitable that there be questions and paradoxes regarding Him.

The reason for all these questions is that G-d is high above our minds, which is correct and proper. If we could understand G-d's ways with our logic, our minds would be like His, heaven forbid. (Likutey Moharan B 52)

The [religious] world thinks that faith is a minor issue, but I consider it an extremely great thing.

The main road to faith is devoid of all sophistication and speculation. It is the innocent faith of the most average individual. (Sichos HaRan 33)

[Rabbi Noson of Nemorov writes:] Rabbi Nachman once told me..."You have faith, but you have no faith in yourself"...

The main lesson here is that you must have faith in yourself. You must believe that you are precious in G-d's eyes. The fact that every single individual is important to Him is a measure of G-d's goodness. (Sichos Haran 140)

Rabbi Nachman once chuckled, "If a single dead soul

were allowed to visit an assembly of secular philosophers, that would be the end of all their teachings." (Sichos Haran 226)

The passage says, "Blessed is the man who trusts in Hashem, and Hashem shall be his trust." (Jeremiah 17:7)

There is a trustor, a trustee, and a trust. The trustor is the person who trusts. The trustee is the one in whom he trusts. The trust is the means in which he trusts to bring about a desired result.

Hashem is the trustee, since [He guarantees] that He will give man everything he needs. He will fulfill all man's desires, if he only walks in Hashem's ways.

Man is the trustor.

The trust is the means through which Hashem gives him a livelihood. Even when a person trusts that Hashem will supply his needs, this still requires some means, be it business, profession, or other source of income.

This, however, is not the true essence of faith. The main concept of faith is that Hashem is alone, and there is nothing with Him. G-d does not need any ways or means through which to give man a livelihood, since He is the way of all ways, and the means of all means.

Therefore, even if a person does not engage in any means whatsoever and does not involve himself in any business or other source of livelihood, Hashem, in His great love, can still provide him with a livelihood.

It is therefore written, "Blessed is the man who trusts in Hashem, and Hashem shall be his trust." (Jeremiah 17:7) His trust shall also be G-d.

G-d then acts alone. Nothing else is required as a means or cause for such a person's livelihood, nor is there anything else that fulfills that in which he trusts. Everything comes from Hashem, and no other ways or means are required.

Even when a person does receive something through some other cause, he should believe with perfect faith that it is literally from Hashem. [He should realize that] Hashem wanted to sustain him in this particular way, but He does not really need these ways and means. This person should then trust only in Hashem. This is a very high level. (Degel Machaneh Ephraim, BeShalach 33c)

There are two aspects of [our understanding of] G-d, namely that He is near and yet far, [imminent and yet transcendental.]

We see G-d as far off and transcendental, since we believe that the blessed Infinite Light is first among the first, and that nothing in the universe can comprehend Him at all. Thought itself cannot grasp G-d, since even thought is something that was created, while G-d is without beginning. Even the highest angel cannot comprehend G-d, as He is higher than all comprehension. This is the concept of G-d as being distant, where He is transcendental and far from our understanding.

At the same time, we also understand G-d to be near, since we believe that He fills all worlds. (Zohar 3:225a) He is contained in all worlds, surrounds all worlds, and no place is empty of Him, as it is written, "The whole earth is filled with His glory." (Isaiah 6:3) This is the concept of G-d's nearness.

We believe in both of these aspects, that G-d is both [imminent and transcendental,] near and yet far.

It is written, "Peace, peace to the one who is far and to the one who is near, says G-d." (Isaiah 17:19) G-d is speaking to the righteous man, who realizes that he is far from G-d, and yet at the same time believes that he is near to Him. Because of such individuals, G-d brings [peace and] all kinds of abundance to the world.

There are two main aspects [of our feeling toward G-d], love and fear. Fear only applies to something that is superior to us. The concept of fear therefore applies to G-d when we think of Him in the transcendental sense, but from the sense that G-d is close, love arises. (Kedushas Levi, Mishpatim p. 139)

Faith is a very strong thing, and it can greatly fortify your life. If you have faith, you have a source of comfort and inspiration, even when trouble strikes. You realize that all troubles are ultimately for your good and can be an atonement for your sins. You know that G-d will be good to you in the end, both in this world and in the next.

The faithless skeptic, on the other hand, has nowhere to turn when troubles strike. He is utterly alone, with neither comfort nor inspiration. (Sichos Haran 32)

Let me conclude by sharing with you a story of a simple man that loved G-d with all his heart.

The Ba'al Shem Tov on one occasion invited his students, "Come, let us go learn a lesson in the love of Hashem."

He escorted them to a nearby open field where a shepherd tended his flock. Spontaneously, the shepherd elevated his voice towards heaven and exclaimed: "Dear Hashem, I love you so! I will dance for You to show You my great love."

With that, the simple shepherd broke into a joyful dance. After finishing his dance, he turned yet again towards the heavens. "Dear *Hashem*, my love for You has no bounds! I will express my love by jumping back and forth across this small pond."

After jumping back and forth for a while, he called heavenward once more: "What can I offer You to prove my deep love for You, Oh *Hashem*! Here, I have a coin in my pocket- I will give it to You." The shepherd took the coin and cast it heavenward. [Some versions of the story relate that the coin did not descend.] (From my Book, A Journey Into Holiness p.34)

You know, all of us whether Jew, B'nei Noach or convert must constantly work on increasing our faith. Once, Elijah was pulled into action from G-d, just to teach a simple Jew some faith.

A certain rich man had a lot of land, but he had no oxen with which to plough it. So, what did he do? He took his wallet full of money and went to another city to the market to purchase some oxen.

It is accurate to say that this man was very generous, giving a lot of charity, and always offering hospitality in his home. However, his heart was not firm in believing in Hashem's Divine providence over all things. After being generous to others, he would often think to himself in a proud way that, "It is my own doing and ability which have brought me all this wealth," for he had made an abundant amount of money.

On his way to the other town, he was met by Elijah the prophet, who was disguised as a peddler going to market. Elijah asked the man, "Where are you going?" He responded that he was going to the market to purchase some oxen. The old man said to him, "Say, *be'ezras* Hashem, G-d willing, or if G-d, blessed be He, so decrees." However, the man gave no heed to the advice, responding "My money is in my wallet and it all depends on my will." Elijah responded, "If that is your attitude, then you are not going to be successful in this."

Not so long after, the rich man's wallet fell out of his pocket without his noticing it. Elijah then picked it up and placed it under a large rock deep in the forest, in a place where no one ever passed.

When the man made a deal for some oxen at the market, and reached for his wallet to pay, he realized that he had misplaced it while traveling and went home in disappointment. Again, he took more money from his safe and went to the market to buy oxen. Once again Elijah the prophet, who was also going to the market, met him. However, this time appearing like a different old man.

Elijah asked him, "Where are you going sir?" The merchant answered that he was going to the market to purchase some oxen. The old man answered back, "Say, *be'ezras* Hashem, G-d willing, or if Hashem, blessed be He, so decrees." However, the man continued his stubbornness, giving the same answer as he did the first time.

Elijah, who was sent from Hashem to fix this man's perspective, caused sleepiness to descend upon him. The merchant sat down to rest and quickly fell into a deep slumber. Then, once asleep, without the merchant feeling anything, Elijah removed his wallet with the money out of his pocket.

He then left it in the middle of the forest for safekeeping, along with the previous funds.

When the merchant awoke, and noticed that his money had disappeared yet again, he said to himself, "It must have been that robbers came along and stole my wallet." Once again, he went home in disappointment.

While repeating his way through the trail home, it finally dawned upon him: "No, this must be Hashem's hand causing this to happen because I haven't believed with complete faith in the Divine Providence of the Creator, blessed be He." So, he decided then and there that from that day forward, he would always say "*be'ezras* Hashem" for everything he planned to do.

So, the merchant tried a third time with his new dedication to Hashem, taking a wallet full of money to go to the market to buy oxen. Again, Elijah met him on the road, this time in the guise of a poor youth who was looking to hire himself out for some work. The boy asked the merchant, "Where is my master going?" He responded happily, "I'm going to the market to buy oxen, *be'ezras* Hashem." Elijah, who was the boy, blessed him with success in his purchase and requested of him, "Let me ask you just one thing, master. When you purchase the oxen and require a helper to drive them to your home, perhaps you'll be kind enough to hire me for the work? I'll be at the market too, and I'm very poor and it's that kind of work that I'm setting my hopes on." The merchant said to him gladly, "Fine, if *be'ezras* Hashem, I buy some oxen, come to me then and I'll take you on to help me drive them home."

The merchant did indeed purchase good oxen, and cheaply too. As promised, he hired Elijah, the boy, to lead the oxen home. While traveling on the road, they were passing alongside the large forest with the oxen, and in the middle of the journey the oxen stampeded, fleeing into the depths of the forest. The merchant and the boy chased after them but, unable to catch up to them, the oxen went farther and farther into the woods. They stopped however, when they came to the crag of the large rock on which the two earlier wallets, with the money, were placed.

Finally, when the merchant caught up with the animals, he noticed his wallets with the money still in them and was overcome with joy. He immediately gave full praise to Hashem, right there and then. Following this, his oxen went along calmly, listening to the commands of those leading them, until finally the merchant returned safely to his home. Then, suddenly, the boy vanished into thin air. The heart of the merchant was opened, and he understood that it was nothing but providence from above that was behind all this. About himself, he said the verse, "It is an ignorant man who will not know, and a fool who will not understand this." (Psalms 92:7) (My Book, Pathways of the Righteous, p. 100)

I think for the new convert or B'nei Noach, faith is so fundamental. Many grew up among other religions which also spoke about faith. However, only Judaism takes faith to such an elevated level. Faith is important but it's not the only thing to serve Hashem with. You can't only preach faith to people, you have to teach them how to study Torah, grow in fear of G-d and love of Him.

I have encountered people who tell me how faithful they are in G-d, yet other than this, they seem to do nothing in the matter of actually being His servant. You can walk into other places of worship and they will preach and preach about their distorted faith, yet other than this, nobody actually does anything. Judaism is based on 613 concepts. For the B'nei Noach, they have seven concepts which expound into many others. To build your faith, you must serve Hashem in all the aspects that He requires of you.

Reb Shlomo Carlebach taught, "The more real a thing is the less you can see it. After you reach the level where you can see all those things which are not to be seen, then you open your eyes, and everything is clear to you, and it feels like you saw it all the time. To love someone is the deepest thing in the world, but you can't prove it. You can't put your finger on it, but it's the most real thing in the world. G-d is the most, utmost real thing in the world, and you can't see Him, but after you don't see Him, you see Him. Then you can see Him everywhere, in every flower, in every cloud, in ever little stone, in every candle. When we say *Shema*, G-d is One, we close our eyes, because first we don't see G-d, we're blind, we just believe, but then we open our eyes and it's so clear, He's always there.

"Everybody likes G-d to do miracles, but the big question is, are you a miracle? If you are living on the level of miracles, if you trust in G-d on the level of a miracle, then miracles happen to you. If you are not living your life on that level, then miracles don't happen to you."

The Kuzari writes, "There is no less wisdom in the creation of the flea or gnat than there is in the creation and orbiting of the heavenly spheres. The distinction between one and the other lies in the substance from which they were created. There is no more purpose in a person's asking, why did He not create me as an angel, than in a worm's asking, why did He not create me as a human being?

The wisdom which is apparent in the spheres is not greater than that in the smallest animals. The spheres (planets) are of a higher form because they were created from matter that is pure and permanent which only their Creator can destroy, while living creatures are made from matter which is highly sensitive and is affected by conflicting influences, such as cold and heat that are constantly exerted against it.

These creatures would have been destroyed in the course of time were it not for G-d's wisdom in creating them as males and females, through which He preserves the species despite the death of individuals." (Kuzari page. 27)

CHAPTER 4:
The Tikkun

When G-d created the world, He created it perfect. His intent was to share His creation and Torah with us. Adam and Chava, whom Hashem chose to create in order to share His Torah with, broke the one commandment that Hashem told them not to break, eating from the *Etz Hadas* (Tree of life). In their human imperfection they reasoned that they wanted to know Hashem better and that eating from the forbidden tree would bring them knowledge to do so. They lacked faith in their Creator and ate, which caused the perfect world they were given to plummet to the world we see today. It has been our job ever since to rectify this broken world through *tikkun*. In brief this entails us following His *mitzvos* and doing His will. When you recognize that there is a *tikkun*, being self-centered is no longer an option. You realize that the very breath you take can be used for good or bad. Your life has more meaning than just living without a purpose.

For some, the idea of *tikkun* seems overwhelming. They are happy enough getting through each day, receiving their pay check and bringing it home to their family. Having some recreation or sport they enjoy, maybe even a hobby. They think, let someone else work on *tikkun*. Why should I become Jewish and have this entire idea of *tikkun* resting on my shoulders?

You might wonder, how did all this get started? To understand, you must go back in history to Adam and Eve. G-d commanded man not to eat from the Tree of Knowledge because man did not have the power to transmit the light of these sparks. Their root was very high, and man could not properly draw down their light. (Etz Chaim, Shaar Rapach

Nitzutzim 2)

As a result of Adam's disobedience, these sparks fell lower and lower, but through the devotion of the righteous, Torah and commandments, these sparks are transported from darkness to light and elevated higher and higher, back to their root and source.

When these sparks are elevated on high, their light is increased, for "light is increased when it emanates from darkness." (Zohar 3:47b) Our sages thus teach us, "In the place where those who repent stand [even the perfectly righteous cannot stand]." (Sanhedrin 99a; Berachos 34b)

This can be understood with a parable. A son was separated from his father, blundering in many crooked ways. Later, when he returned to his father, there was all the more joy.

G-d therefore said, "On the day that you eat from it you will die." It was on that day alone that the concept of death would be transmitted. Eating of the Tree of Knowledge would cause the sparks to descend and fall lower and lower, to be clothed in the physical garments of the "Glowing Husk." This lowering is the concept of death.

[This concept of death was only for that one day.] Later, through the devotion of the righteous, through Torah and commandments, this darkness would be transformed into light. The sparks would then rise higher and higher to their root and source, causing even greater delight.

Before the sin, Adam and Chava did not yet comprehend the concept of separating and elevating the sparks. They therefore did not understand that G-d was only speaking of a temporary death. Assuming that G-d was speaking of permanent death, they questioned His statement, since the Tree was created with G-d's word, which is the source of life.

Having this question, they thought that G-d's intent was that the Tree of Knowledge contained such great light that they could not tolerate it, and therefore should not transmit it to themselves. It would then be like the case of the four who entered Paradise [where one died, one lost his reason, one lost his faith, and only one emerged whole. (Chagigah 14b) Their assumption was that the tree was dangerous, but not deadly.]

In quoting G-d's commandment, the woman therefore said, "lest you die." It was only a possibility and not a certainty. It was possible that they would not be fit to perceive and tolerate it, and as a result, it was possible that they would transmit to themselves an aspect of death. They had also anticipated the serpent's question, and therefore had this doubt.

The serpent therefore replied, "You will not die." He asserted that there was not even any question, saying, "You will certainly not die. You are on a high enough level to tolerate even such great light. This is especially true, because when you eat of it, 'you will be like G-d.'" (Genesis 3:5)

The serpent thus convinced them that they would rise to such a prominent level that they would be fit to receive and tolerate even such a great light. This was the manner in which the serpent tricked them. Understand this. (Kedushas Levi, Bereshis p.7,8)

There are sparks of light hidden in this world. Some you can find and liberate: When you "Know G-d in all your ways" (Proverbs 3:6) - finding Him in whatever you do, those sparks jump out at you and their light is released, but then there are sparks of such intensity that they had to be buried in the deepest bowels of the material realm and locked away in thick darkness. There are sparks that no ordinary search could uncover. Your intellect has no power even to approach them. Your deeds could never dig that deep. Your eyes would be blinded by their brilliance and by the profundity of the darkness surrounding them.

The only tools you have to liberate those sparks are the ones that supersede your intellect and your senses. These are the inner powers that are revealed when you withstand a test of faith.

This is the reason we find our faith tested again and again in this generation: We are redeeming the final sparks of light. (Bringing Heaven down to Earth p. 89)

G-d willed that He would have pleasure when the other side is subdued, and when darkness is transformed into light. (Zohar 1:4a) The places of darkness and the other side in this physical world are then illuminated with the Infinite Light of G-d, with even more intensity and strength.

This is the light that emerges from darkness. (Zohar 3:47) It is even greater than the light of the higher [spiritual] universes. [In the higher worlds] this light only shines through garments and through a concealment of their presence. This screens the light of the Infinite Being, hiding it so that the existence [of these upper worlds] should not be nullified.

It is for this reason that G-d gave us the Torah. The Torah is called "strength and power." (Shir HaShirim Rabbah 2:10; Zohar 2:58a, 3:269a, Zevachim 116a) [This "strength" is alluded to in the teaching of] our sages, which states that G-d gives the righteous the power to accept their reward in the ultimate future. (Sanhedrin 100b)

This is necessary in order that their existence not be utterly nullified in the light of G-d that will ultimately be revealed without any [coverings or] garments whatsoever. It is thus written, "Your Teacher will no longer hide Himself... but your eyes shall behold your Teacher." (Isaiah 30:20) It is also written, "For eye to eye will they see [G-d returning to Zion]." (Isaiah 52:8) It is furthermore written, "G-d shall be to you for an everlasting light..." (Isaiah 60:19)

It is known that the culmination and fulfillment of creation will take place in the days of the Messiah, and particularly, after the resurrection of the dead. It was for this reason that the world was initially created. (Tanya 36 (45b))

Finding your place inside the *tikkun* is not so complicated. Every good action you do, even just recognizing G-d's hand in a situation, brings a *tikkun*. Every B'nei Noach, when they do kindness to others, are making a *tikkun*. How? All light comes from Hashem to the Jewish people, and then that light is dispersed among the nations. It says in the Talmud, during the rain, Israel is watered first and then the water descends to the other countries and nations.

Any good deed around the world is triggered from some Jew doing a *mitzvah* or learning Torah. When it says that we are a light upon the nations, it means literally. The Torah and *mitzvos* of the Jewish people are vital for the world's existence, but you too are connected to this light through them.

The Baal Shem Tov was once immersing in the nearby lake as a *mikvah*. A non-Jew saw him break the ice and enter therein. Fearing this holy man becoming cold, he ran over and placed towels down for when the rabbi would ascend. The Baal Shem Tov then blessed him with long life and thanked him for his actions. The man later lived well over 100 years.

People always make jokes how the world is run by the Jews. How the financial banks, politicians all have Jewish sponsors pressuring them to act in their benefit. Well, not only is this true, but it reaches far deeper than this. The Talmud says that G-d gave the Jewish sages the keys to the world. This is no joke. There were times in history when the sages could have ushered in the Messiah before his time, that is how much power Hashem gave them. However, they chose not to. Why? Because the world would have experienced too much suffering and wars should he have arrived then. It is the Jewish sages that uphold all the world. That is why it's so important to respect and support the sages.

I don't know if you have ever met a true sage. It is quite an experience. These rabbis are wise beyond anything you can imagine. Thousands of pages of Torah, they have committed to memory. They understand life like you cannot imagine. The world is so clear to them, if only more people would listen to their advice. I think that is one of the problems with newcomers to Judaism. They don't realize how each Jewish group have their own personal rabbi and sages that they follow. Even if what the rabbi advises you doesn't make sense, his advice comes with a blessing from G-d that always seems to work out in the end. That is why it is so important to choose a main rabbi to convert you, one who is so inclined to see the greater picture behind situations. Then to not only ask advice but to actually heed to it. This is part of your faith in G-d, that you trust in His leaders to guide you.

CHAPTER 5:
Having a Choice

An individual once asked [Rabbi Nachman] to define free will. He replied, "The definition is simple. Free will is the ability to do something if you want to, and the ability to refrain from something if you so desire."

[Rabbi Nathan writes:] I recorded this, for it contained a very necessary lesson. Some people are very perplexed regarding this. They are very habituated in their ways and deeds from their youth, and they think that they no longer have the free will to change their ways. This is everything. He can do whatever he desires. Understand this well. (Likutey Moharan B 110)

Whenever you do anything to divorce yourself from the mundane world, all powers come to help you. This is true whenever you need it, whenever there is any pressure or trouble.

Rabbi Akiva said, "All is foreseen, but permission is given." (Mishnah Avos 3:15) This means that even though Hashem already knows the outcome on what will be, we have free will in order to change things from our perspective.

Every creation has its role to play - and just as the trees cannot complain and say, "It is only fair that we, who out number humans, should be given the ability to fulfill the Torah", no animals or human can either. If someone was created as a cow, there is a reason; if they were created as a tree, there is a reason; creations have no right to decide what role they play - G-d decides what's best for them and the world.

Know that man must cross over [this world] on a very, very narrow bridge. The main thing is not to be afraid at all. (Likutey Moharan B 48)

It is not the individual who fears, but something else inside them. A person may clearly realize that the thing that they fear cannot harm them, but still, they cannot help being terrified by it. This is because something within them is causing this fear. We actually see that many people have ridiculous phobias, and even though they realize the foolishness of their fears, they still cannot overcome them.

When we suddenly shout behind a person's back, they become startled. They exhibit fear even before they know what is causing it. They can have fear without it entering their conscious mind. Fear is not in the conscious, so it does not have to be rational. This is because the fear actually stems from something else within the individual.

The same is true of desire. A person may realize that their desire is utter foolishness, but it still remains strong. Here again, it is not the person who desires, but something else within them. Even if they are aware of the foolishness of their desire, this something else continues to want it.

If you learn to understand yourself, you can rid yourself of all fears and desire. You must simply realize that something else within you is responsible for them. Understand this, and you can overcome everything.

You have free will. You can easily train your mind to avoid that thing within you that is responsible for your fears and desires. (Sichos Haran 83)

A person is similar to a bounty hunter. They were brought into this world in order to recapture the escaped sparks and return them. What is most remarkable about this is that even those farthest from Hashem have been assigned this task. In fact, when those far from Hashem repent and do His will, they are able to capture the most sparks. This is because they are returning from a low place where most fallen sparks have accumulated. That is why the Talmud says the *ba'al teshuva* is able to reach a higher level than the sage who is untainted by sins. This is why the convert to Judaism has such a great responsibility on his shoulders to convert properly. (My Book, The True Intentions of the Baal Shem Tov)

"Rebbe Pinchas of Koretz taught that a holy spark falls and burns inside a *ger* (convert to Judaism). It compels him to complete his *geirus* (conversion) and actually does not give him any choice in this matter. Only after his *geirus* is the *ger* given free choice."

G-d can do anything. He could even, as the saying goes, "fit an elephant through the eye of a needle." So, how would He do it? Would He make the elephant smaller? Or would He expand the eye of the needle. Illogical? True, but logic is just another of His creations. He who created logic is permitted to disregard it. (Bringing Heaven down to Earth, p. 46)

Imagine: Hashem tells the water, "Create a flood. In this-and-this place. These four people are to die. These six others are to be injured. That is part of the destiny of the world."

But the wind answers: "No. I refuse. I don't want those people dead."

Of course, that cannot happen. Nothing can rebel against Hashem, or rather, almost nothing. The Shulchan Aruch is a force of nature. We, the Jews, were given the job to make the Shulchan Aruch work. The only difference between us and the angel of water, is that we do have the ability to be stupid enough to thwart Hashem's plan.

People die every day. Entire nations go extinct. Nobody has a problem with that because they know that's nature, that's the world, that's destiny. What you need to understand is that Hashem runs the world through the Shulchan Aruch as well, and we Jews are guardians of His plan. Hashem could destroy Amalek with a flood, with an earthquake, or with a volcano, but He chose a different way. It's up to us to carry it out.

R. Akiva Eiger zt"l writes that when the nations refused to accept the Torah, not every single member of every single nation refused. Most did. In general, they did, but there were individuals who did want to accept it. Those individuals, says R. Akiva Eiger, become converts.

Regardless of whether someone is called "Israel", they

are still given a mission by G-d, that is, to fulfill the seven Noachide Laws. Everyone's a soldier, Jewish or not.

Reb Shlomo Carlebach told, "I want to learn a little bit from the holy Baal Shem Tov on truth. I just want to bless you with it. The first thing is, a person has to make up his mind, I want to tell the truth, and I don't ever want to lie. And then G-d will help him, and whatever he does will be true because we always think, I'm just telling a lie, but my life is truth. It's not true. If I utter words of lies, then I become a liar. My life becomes a lie, and even the truth I say is also a lie. You know you don't have to lie. Sometimes you tell the truth and you're lying. So therefore, the Baal Shem Tov says if you're strong, you don't ever want to lie, then everything you do becomes real.

This is very deep. Anything you do for the sake of G-d cannot be done with your lying because let's say, for instance, when I'm doing something for the sake of G-d, that means I'm giving G-d a gift. When you give somebody a gift, it has to have a little page, a little wrapping, right? The gift, when you do something for G-d, the wrapping has to be in truth. It simply must be in truth.

The holy Baal Shem Tov says, a lot of people don't lie in their words, but they're lying in their thoughts and they're lying deep down in their souls. So, he says you should be ready to die, G-d forbid, when you lie to yourself and your soul. It's much easier not to lie to people; not lying to yourself is the hardest thing in the world. It says there is nothing in the world G-d says to keep away from. He just rather says, 'Just don't do it.' You know, let's say, not to eat ham or pig, it's forbidden to eat it, but G-d doesn't say keep away from it. It's forbidden to eat it, right? Keep *Shabbos*. It doesn't say keep away from not keeping *Shabbos*. But for lying, G-d is begging me, please don't lie. On a simple level it means, if I had a friend who is lying, I'd say he's lying, and I'm not lying, but if you're close to people who are lying...

Reb Zusha says something very deep. One word of lying makes you a stranger to G-d. It's hard to talk to a stranger.

With every lie you utter, you become a stranger to G-d. The most horrible thing in the world. Can you imagine if the greatest thing in the world becomes a stranger to you?

There is an open truth and a hidden truth. You know sometimes it's so deep, so true, it's completely interior. This is the deepest, holiest truth in the world. The most hidden thing in the world is G-d. The most hidden thing in the world is to love people because it's so true. Anything that is so true, is hidden. It's hidden, and it's very holy.

I want you to know something very deep. Some parents tell their child, 'I could do without you.' When the child grows up, he thinks, 'G-d could do without me,' or, 'The world could do without me.' How can you be a Jew unless it's clear to you that G-d can't do without you?" (Open your Heart p.125-227)

There is a prophesy. It is coming true today. "Days are coming... There will be a hunger in the world; but the hunger will not be for bread and the thirst will not be for water; but to hear the word of the living G-d." (Amos 8:11)

"There is a saying that everything in the world is here for the service of G-d. Somebody once came to Reb Alexander and asked him how can you serve Hashem by being an atheist? Reb Alexander answered that you have to be an atheist when someone asks a favor from you. If you believe in G-d, then deep down you'll think, 'I'll pray for you, I'll bless you, but I don't have to do anything, because G-d will do it.' So, when someone asks a favor of you, my most beautiful friends, you have to be a complete atheist because G-d won't do anything for him, you have got to do it!

"Sometimes, someone asks a favor which is very hard. We don't have the faintest idea what a favor the person is doing us by asking! At that very moment G-d is opening gates for us, giving us a chance to have the image of G-d on our face again. We have to wash and polish ourselves, but sometimes there is so much dirt that soap and water aren't enough, we have to rub and scratch the dirt off. Even that isn't enough sometimes, and we have to go to a sauna. You have to do a *mitzvah* on the level of a sauna, burning hot. Sweat it out." (Holy Brother, p. 155)

Rabbi Noson Maimon once said that people are upset when someone comes to them asking for money. What they don't realize is that G-d is desiring closeness to you. Should you do the kindness, He will then reciprocate by sending you your desires. When you reject him, not performing this act of kindness, you reject Hashem's goodness. Therefore, think twice before you turn a blind eye to your brother in pain. Always remember to emulate G-d and do kindness to others.

CHAPTER 6:
Joy and Sadness

You might wonder why I have included a chapter on the topic of joy. Well, throughout the years, I have noticed converts struggling with depression and anxiety. It is so common that it must be addressed.

It is almost as if during the transition between B'nei Noach and conversion, a switch is turned on and a more complex emotional battle pursues. Possibly potential converts are coming into the conversion with baggage that they haven't dealt with, thinking that Judaism will solve their problems. I really wish I could remove this pain from the converts life. Maybe by addressing it before the conversion it will help a little?

The main thing is that you should always be happy. This is especially true when you are bound to G-d. Without joy, it is impossible to be attached constantly to G-d. (Likutey Yekarim 2b)

The main rule in serving G-d is that you should keep yourself from sadness and depression to the very best of your ability. (Likkutey Yakarim 1b)

Rabbi Menachem Mendel Schneerson writes, "Depression is not a crime, but it plummets a person into an abyss deeper than any crime could reach. Depression is a ploy instigated by the self-destructive elements within all of us. Once depressed, a person could do anything.

"Fight depression as a blood sworn enemy. Run from it as you would run from death itself." (Bringing Heaven down to Earth p. 94)

In today's era, depression and anxiety are

commonplace. However, I noticed this issue among converts, decades ago. I believe the Satan specifically tries to make converts suffer in this way. He figures, if they are sad, they will reevaluate being Jewish. He thinks, "I will do everything in my power to make them sad so that they isolate themselves from the Jewish community and return to their previous lifestyle."

Rabbi Menachim Mendel of Vitebsk says, "Depression is the strongest impurity of all. We thus find that idolatry is called by a similar name. [The Hebrew word for sadness and depression is *atzav*, and the same word is used for idolatry] as we find, 'Their idols (*atzav-eyhem*) are silver and gold, [the work of human hands].' (Psalms 115:4)

"Depression thus has no relationship to G-d. Regarding G-d it is written, 'Force and joy are in His place.' (Chronicles 16:27) 'The Divine Presence therefore only rests on a place of joy.'" (Shabbos 30b) (Pri HaAretz, Matos-Masai 28b)

When you are happy and at peace, it is easy to set aside some time each day to express your thoughts before G-d with a broken heart, but when you are depressed, it is very difficult to isolate yourself and speak to G-d. You must therefore force yourself to always be happy, especially during prayer.

Rabbi Nachman said that true happiness is one of the most difficult things to achieve in serving G-d. Another time, he said that it seems impossible to achieve happiness without some measure of foolishness. One must resort to all sorts of humor if this is the only way to obtain happiness. When a person attains true joy, G-d Himself watches him and protects him from defilement. (Sichos Haran 20)

Depression is like anger and rage. It is a complaint against G-d for not fulfilling your wishes.

When you have a broken heart, you are like a child pleading before your father. You are like a baby crying and complaining because your father is far away. (Sichos Haran 42)

Reb Shlomo Carlebach taught, "The less joy you have, the less you are one with someone else. Sad people are not one with each other: Everybody is sitting in a corner moping by themselves.

"The more you are filled with joy, the more you can be together with somebody else. So, when people say they want to get married, all their friends come together to make themselves crazy with joy, in order to put them together. And it's the same between us and G-d. Unless you are filled with joy, you are not one with G-d.

"Rebbe Nachman says, 'How much would you give not to stop breathing? You have to give a million times more in order not to stop being happy.'

"We are human beings We are sometimes sad, and sometimes we are 100% right to be sad, but the most important thing is that even when you are sad, don't lose hope.

"You are sad? You are 100% right, but have you ever been happy about the things you do have? Why are you so sad? Because there is something missing in your life. But you are alive. Let's start from there. Why don't you dance for one week just because you are alive?

"Everybody believes in G-d, hopefully. But do you know how much G-d believes in us? The world still exists. That means that G-d believes in us; believes that we can fix everything." (Open your Hearts p.120, p.31, p. 28)

"People walk around sad because they don't know what to do with their future. You have this minute right now. What are you doing with it? The difference between sadness and joy is very simple. Sadness always tells you: 'Oy vey! What are you going to do in ten minutes? What will you do ten years from now?' If you are really filled with joy for one minute, then you will know what to do the next minute also. What is G-d giving you? He is giving you this minute. He hasn't given tomorrow. Of course, I don't know what to do tomorrow because I didn't receive it yet. Sadness is very much concerned with what I don't have, and I really don't have tomorrow yet. The truth is, I am always standing before nothingness because I am non-existent yet for the next minute. I'm not here yet. Time isn't there. The world isn't there. The world is here... right now!" (Holy Brother p.37)

So, let's make the best of things. Let's take time out each day to list all the good things in our life and thank Hashem for them. There is so much hope, don't ever let the Satan convince you differently. Be proud of your accomplishments. Appreciate the specialness of your soul.

CHAPTER 7:
Ilovetorah Mindfulness

Ilovetorah Mindfulness, by Reb Moshe, is a form of Jewish meditation that combines classical western and eastern meditation methods (which are diluted methods of original Jewish, Kabbalah meditation) based on Jewish Torah values and Kabbalah. The main difference between regular mindfulness and ilovetorah Mindfulness is the idea of *tikkun*, rectification. While the non-Jewish method of mindfulness would be to simply observe one's thoughts, I teach that no thought is there by accident, and so must be given a *tikkun* and be elevated back to its source. We understand from Kabbalah that man was put on this earth to elevate all of mankind and the world. Combining his knowledge in Jewish meditation, Talmud, Kabbalah, and NLP (Neuro-linguistic programming, NLP, is an approach to communication, personal development, and psychotherapy), I seek to give a new direction to mindfulness meditation.

Mindfulness is a state of active, open attention on the present moment. When you're being mindful, you observe your thoughts and feelings from a distance, without judging them as good or bad. When practicing mindfulness, one becomes aware of their "stream of consciousness", and instead of letting life pass you by, you will come to live in the moment. Thoughts come and go of their own accord. You are not your thoughts, but thoughts are given to you by both the Satan and *Hashem* to challenge you. They will come and go, and ultimately you have a choice about whether to act on them or not. The Baal Shem Tov says, "A person is where his thoughts are." By just observing thoughts that come to you, choosing only the good ones, and elevating the negative, harmful thoughts back to their source in the *Sefiros* (upper worlds), you thereby elevate them and the world. You release yourself from thought patterns before they tip you into a downward emotional spiral. This begins the process of putting you back in control of your life.

Mindfulness training may:

1. **Improve memory and academic performance** (PsyBlog). In this study, students who did attention-building exercises experienced increased focus (or less mind-wandering), better short-term memory, and better performance on exams.

2. **Help with weight loss and a healthier diet.** Mindful eating means paying attention to each bite and eating slowly while paying attention to all your senses (Harvard Medical School, Women's Health). Participants in mindfulness studies ate fewer calories when they were hungrier than the regular groups.

3. **Lead to better decision-making.** Mindfulness reduces our tendency to stick with lost causes—such as an unhealthy relationship or dead-end job—because of the time and energy already invested (BPS Research).

4. **Lower stress and help cope with chronic health issues.** Mindfulness increased the mental and physical well-being in patients diagnosed with chronic pain, cancer, heart disease, and more (Elsevier).

5. **Improve immunity and create positive brain changes.** Researchers measured brain activity before and after volunteers were trained in mindfulness meditation for eight weeks, finding positive changes in brain activity (Psychosomatic Medicine).

6. **Other brain benefits we've seen from mindfulness meditation:** Better focus, more creativity, less anxiety and depression, and more compassion for others.

BELOW ARE SOME STEPS OFTEN DONE IN MINDFULNESS TRAINING:

(a) Use a consistent posture or place of meditation.

(b) Try to distinguish between naturally arising thoughts and elaborated thinking.

(c) Focus on current feelings of the body in order to release tension.

(d) Follow your breath as an anchor for attention during meditation.

(e) Repeatedly count up and down to ten consecutive inhalations and exhalations.

(f) Label the thoughts that come to you; don't suppress the occurrence of thoughts.

KABBALISTIC MINDFULNESS, ILOVETORAH METHOD:

(a) Combine Rebbe Nachman's *hisbodidus* methods with Mindfulness.

(b) Try to gently let go of thoughts and elevate them for their *Tikkun,* rectification in the *Sefiros* (Explained in my book, Chassidus Kabbalah & Meditation).

(c) Add *emunah,* faith that all thoughts and all tests, in one's life, come from *Hashem* and are there to help us grow.

(d) Use Hypnotic Anchoring to train our subconscious (Establishing a trigger which, when activated, will trigger certain responses; this happens randomly in life, but can be suggested during hypnosis).

(e) Carefully use permitted Kabbalistic names in order to increase healing and fear of *Hashem* (like focusing on *YKVK*). This is only permitted once your converted to Judaism. (Explained in my book, Chassidus Kabbalah & Meditation)

MINDFULNESS AND STRESS RELIEF

Most of us experience stress in our lives one way or another. Studies show that mindfulness can help you to stop focusing on things that cause stress. It prevents you from dwelling on negative thoughts over and over. Mindfulness can be used to decrease anxiety about the present, as well as the future. It can allow you to take a mental break from stressful thoughts, leading to better health.

The regular practice of mindfulness meditation leads

to a complete change in your perspective. Mindfulness is more than a simple meditative technique. It is a way of life. After a while, you will find yourself practicing mindfulness subconsciously while gardening, listening to music and even while cleaning the house. Focus on the present and quiet the voice that offers a running commentary on what you're doing, what you've done, and what you will be doing. You can start living a life with true perspective. It truly is time to take our lives back and not over- think.

How to Start Mindfulness

Week 1

Sit in a relaxing and quiet place.

Practice taking deep breaths and counting from one to ten, then reverse the count from ten to one. Do this for ten to fifteen minutes. Pay attention to your stomach muscles while inhaling and exhaling.

Week 2

Continue your practice of taking deep breaths, but this time try doing so without needing to count.

Start to label the sensations that you feel. For instance, if you hear something, label that as a sound. If you smell an odor, label that as a smell. Should you have a thought, label that as a thought, and you can either think about this or release it, let it go. Do this with all senses, thoughts, and feelings.

Week 3

Make a set time to meditate, using *hisbodidus* and mindfulness meditation together. They can go together very well, as both are founded on the principle of spontaneous thoughts and sensations.

Practice throughout the day during regular activities, to identify feelings and to just observe them or elevate them.

Advanced Methods

Once you're comfortable with being mindful, you can add numerous Kabbalistic concepts into your meditation. These are explained

85

as well as other methods in my book, Chassidus Kabbalah & Meditation. (Practical and meditative kabbalah is not meant for B'nei Noach or those first involved in the conversion process.)

Remember that mindfulness is not just a meditative practice. It is a way of life, devoid of stress. The Hornosyple Rebbe once told me, "The trials of life are much easier than the stress that comes from overcomplicating, by living events repeatedly in our minds." We have to simply do our best in this world and not drive ourselves crazy unnecessarily.

Mindfulness is about letting go, and not allowing physical feelings to confuse you, by combining meditating on holy names, *hisbodedus,* and using main stream mindfulness methods.

As spoken previously, the goal of all *mitzvos*, prayer, and study is to be connected to *Hashem*. This means being mindful that *Hashem* is always there in all instances of your life.

How do we generally connect to *Hashem*? Through our thoughts and keeping the *mitzvos*. Yes, we pray and make a motion of the mouth, but the main part of prayer is the contemplation and *kavanah* we have in mind. Therefore, getting control of one's mind is a necessity. A loose mind leads to sinful thoughts and actions.

As an opposing view to always being mindful, you have the Kotzker Rebbe who said that one should completely place themselves inside the moment of the *mitzvos*. It isn't enough to look outside oneself to possibly habitually perform the commandments. We have to live completely inside the moment in our thoughts and our feelings. If you're an overthinker, being mindful could cause a bit more stress at times. Every technique requires balance. A wise person serves Hashem in all ways. He takes out only the beneficial parts of wisdom that benefits his particular soul.

CHAPTER 8:
Where to go

The foundational principles of Judaism are based on the observance of the *Shabbos*, keeping *kosher*, as well as modesty laws. Our rituals are learned from an early age in Jewish schools and through observing one's parents keeping the traditions. Children and adults grow up attending synagogues with other congregants. They observe the rabbis and their peers serving Hashem. Experiencing the Torah lifestyle over an extended period, being surrounded by Jews and Judaism is fundamental in keeping the commandments.

The Torah teaches us that we are together, one nation and that we are responsible for one another. Therefore, it is of the utmost importance that your life is defined by synagogue attendance and by having a rabbi that you can learn hands on how to follow the *mitzvos*.

It seems all too easy today to learn everything from books and online classes, but nothing compares to the hands-on experience of surrounding yourself with the Jewish people. Judaism cannot be learned entirely from books, and it was never meant to be self-taught. I encourage people to primarily learn in person with a rabbi and together with other potential converts. Don't attempt to teach yourself Judaism.

A lot of people that want to convert are located in all four corners of the world. They may not have access to personal learning, so it's understandable that they would want to study online. However, this is not the proper way to learn about Judaism, and I must reiterate that Judaism must be experienced. You have various rabbis attempting to give online classes as their business and maybe the money mistakenly convinces them that this is the way to make converts, however it's not. That is what makes Judaism so special, it is a spiritual experience that cannot be explained through mere words, so lofty is it. The more difficult the conversion, the greater the light that needed to be returned from the forces of impurity.

Making converts is a huge responsibility. Most of the time people convert before they are truly ready. Just because a person may be keeping the basic requirements does not mean that they are emotionally ready to become Jewish. Only through years of study and patience will you truly be prepared for this great accomplishment. I would estimate the average proper conversion to take approximately five years or more. I know of cases where people studied for eight years before the rabbi felt they were ready. I also know of cases where people converted properly in two years, however, they were studying on their own for decades prior to meeting the rabbi. However, in that case, the person who converted quickly really struggled after their conversion. It would have been far better to have taken things slowly, then they could have surrounded themselves within the Jewish community, build Jewish friendships and only then to have converted with a supportive community around them.

To begin your studies, you might want to contact an Orthodox synagogue that is local to you. It is very common that people convert through the Lubavitch or Breslav communities (if you seek a Chassidic path) due to their warmth towards newcomers. These two communities seem to be very open-minded towards newcomers and the teachings from their rebbes are especially warm to converts. It is very common that there are already conversion classes taking place in your area. Major cities are often hot stops for outreach centers of Jewish studies. Just be sure that they teach orthodox conversion only.

You might feel alarmed at first, when you are rejected by the local rabbi in your community. This is not uncommon, in fact it is encouraged by the Torah to push away those who wish to convert. As I said before, the Jewish people do not go after the other nations to convert them. We wish to separate out those who are just curious from those who truly have the potential to become Jews.

Most people who begin the conversion process do not complete it, or they take a shortcut and don't convert properly. Therefore, they are never truly Jewish. That is why we must reject people at first and only if they persevere, insisting that this is truly their calling, do we begin to teach them the Jewish ways.

This is not the case however with the Reform and Conservative movement of Judaism. As long as you enjoy Judaism it doesn't matter to them how much you practice the commandments or if you accept only a few laws of your choosing. Here is a good lesson for you in life. Reb Shlomo Carlebach says, "If you do not do something in life giving it 100% of your effort, you're not really doing it." The same holds true with converting to Judaism. If you're not in it for the full experience, then why are you here? If you're confused whether you want to become Jewish or not, then just close the book and move on in life. No one is forcing you to read this or wants you to drastically change your entire lifestyle, even Hashem does not require this of you. He's happy if you just performed the seven laws of Noah, which most people already struggle or reject.

You could spend your entire lifetime just learning to practice the seven laws in order to perfect them. You can be a light unto the nations just from observing these laws. I have been personally inspired by every Noahide that I come upon. Their love for G-d, His people and for Israel is remarkable.

With each Jew that you meet, you have opportunities to inspire them through your own personal yearnings for truth. You have countless Jewish charity organizations that would love your assistance. There's so much you can do to participate and help out the Jewish people that there really is no reason to convert unless the yearning to be completely Jewish is truly inherent in your heart.

In fact, for most people, it would be much preferred

that they didn't pursue conversion because to convert properly, you have to change your clothing, your mindset, you might lose friendships and family members. You might have to quit your job because of *Shabbos* observance. It could be that you might have to even relocate to a new city and walk away from everything you have ever known. You must search deep within your heart to feel the soul inside you and understand its yearnings. Look deep into your life, your family and friends. See past the present and envision yourself years down the line, deciding who you truly want to be. Decide what is truly most important to you.

I know people that left marriages and relationships just to become Jewish. I know converts who cry every day of their life because even after they converted, they feel terribly lonely. Converting and becoming Jewish is not a band aid to your emotional problems. In fact, it will make your life more difficult. It is not something to run away to, should life be difficult. It is something completely pure and it must be motivated with the right desires.

Even while pursuing an Orthodox proper conversion, you may find yourself drawn to a congregation or rabbi that may not be the best influence to complete your conversion. There are many styles and types of Jews from all walks of life. We have Ashkenazic Jews, we have Sephardic Jews and other types inside the Orthodox movement such as Chassidic or Litvish. Choosing which style of Orthodoxy, you prefer is not important at the beginning of your studies. You can decide this later as you gain wisdom and experience. The rabbi that helps you to convert might push you and influence you to follow his direction, but that may not be the best thing for you. However, it's fine to choose a temporary path knowing that you can decide later which movement of Orthodoxy is best for you.

I always encourage those who are studying for conversion to focus on the main works and *halachos*, Jewish laws which they will need in order to live. I urge them not to get lost too much in Jewish literature and philosophy, but to remain focused on what's truly important for them at this time.

Obviously, people need some spirituality, so it will be common for people to desire these other works, but their study should be limited. In the same way, I discourage my fellow Jews from learning things that are extreme for them at their current level. So, this is not just advice for someone who is converting. You must see yourself in the mirror and understand exactly where you're at in life, studying accordingly.

You're going to have to pray a lot in order to accomplish this. Not just through toil alone will you accomplish your needs, but you will require Hashem to be with you the entire time as you embark on this journey. You must call to Him and praise Him often for His guidance.

Too many people are trying to convert by themselves because they feel uncomfortable going to classes or approaching an Orthodox rabbi. When the Jewish people received the Torah on Mount Sinai, we received it from our teacher Moses together, we didn't just open books and study ourselves. We also weren't given the choice to pick and choose which commandments we wanted to observe or which ones we wanted to reject. If that's your attitude when it comes to Judaism, then this is a huge mistake. However, don't be alarmed, you can take your time learning the *mitzvos* and convert when you're ready.

You must understand what it will be required of you to do this transformation. You must realize that you can't stay in your current location if there are no Orthodox synagogues locally for you to attend. You will have to move and possibly change jobs if that's what it takes to surround yourself with Judaism. If you have an excellent job that currently pays well, you might have to take some economic loss in order to make the proper move into a Jewish community.

Please be wise though, and research well the community and people you are going to surround yourself with before you move there. Just because there is an Orthodox shul, it doesn't mean it's the right community for you. Make sure that they are the type of people who will give you the encouragement you're going to need. Always surround yourself with positive people and a good environment. Certainly, you will need a huge amount of encouragement because your non-Jewish family and friends will most certainly discourage you and try to get you to turn back from this journey. To be quite honest, they're not wrong in telling you to return to the lifestyle you grew up with. They would be wrong however if they told you to return back to their religion of idolatry.

You will see how quickly they turn into missionaries for Christianity, Islam or whichever religion they practice once they hear that you actually want to convert to Judaism. You'll be very surprised at how far they will go in order to prevent you from embarking on this journey. You'll be surprised how many of your friends and family actually have animosity towards Jews. The sweet relative you thought you knew might turn into the biggest anti-Semite. If they could, they would probably lock you up in an insane asylum for even considering Judaism. It's important to understand the path that you're about to take. If you don't have the emotional strength, the boldness and the perseverance, then nor will you have the strength to overcome the obstacles that await you.

"When a proselyte comes to be converted, one receives him with an open hand so as to bring him under the wings of the Divine Presence." (Leviticus Rabbah 2:9)

My dear friends I wish I could tell you that we were the sweetest nation in the world at all times. However, if this were the case, the Messiah would already be here. I'll admit to you we have much to work on in order to bring the final redemption. Therefore, I must warn you that not all converts are treated with the dignity they deserve and that we are commanded to give them. It says in the Torah, "You must understand the feelings of the convert." (Exodus 23:9)

I just want you to be prepared for reality. We will have to answer to Hashem should we not treat converts with the proper respect they deserve. The Torah teaches us that we are to welcome them with open hands and to make them part of our family. That we should take care of their every need so that they feel comforted and that they should feel like our equal. However, instead many converts suffer a lot because they feel they are never truly accepted. If I could, I'd fix every communities problem, but things take time to fix, as you know.

Even though we may fail at times at appreciating the convert, that's not the case in Heaven. He cherishes the convert and appreciates such a person that has given up so much in order to come close to Him. As it says, "Beloved are proselytes by G-d, for the Bible everywhere uses the same epithet of them as of Israel." (Talmud, Gerim 4:3)

I wonder if when you attempt to convert, you will come upon a Hillel or a Shamai. Let me share with you a few stories.

We learn in the Talmud some interesting stories of potential converts. A non-Jew once came in front of Shamai; he asked, "how many Torah's do you have?" Shamai responded, "We have two, a written and oral Torah." The potential convert answered, "I believe you about the written Torah, but not about the oral Torah - convert me on condition that you will teach only the written Torah to me!" Shamai angrily drove him away.

Maybe you have already met a local rabbi that similarly drove you away and told you that he didn't think you were ready to convert. This too is from Hashem. Each rejection in life is not for nothing. We grow from them and improve. You can take it as a sign to give up or you can accept it as part of your spiritual journey.

The story continues that the non-Jew didn't give up so fast. He came in front of Hillel; Hillel converted him. The first day, Hillel taught him *alef, beis, gimel, daled* (the Hebrew alphabet); the next day, Hillel reversed the order of the letters.

Caught by surprise, the non-Jew stated, "Yesterday you taught differently! Wisely Hillel proclaimed, "You rely on me to know the letters - you can also rely on me regarding oral Torah!" (Talmud *Shabbos* 31a)

On another occasion, a non-Jew confronted the holy Shamai; he requested conversion on condition that Shamai teach him the entire Torah while standing on one foot - Shamai drove him away with the builder's rod.

Wanting to still convert, he came before the notoriously patient Hillel requesting the same way to convert as he told Shamai. Hillel responded, "Do not do to your friend what is hateful to you (Rashi - do not transgress Hashem's words, like you do not like people who transgress your words), the rest is commentary - go learn!"

Once a potential convert was walking outside a synagogue and heard the *parshah* (weekly Torah portion) of *bigdei kohein hagadol* (clothes worn by the high priest) read from the Torah; he was told that the *kohein hagadol*, high priest, wears them. He came in front of Shamai; he requested conversion on condition to be appointed the *kohein hagadol* - Shamai drove him away with the builder's rod.

He then approached Hillel to convert him [on the same condition]; Hillel did so. (Note: The Maharsha explains that Hillel began to teach the non-Jew but did not convert him until he realized that he cannot be *kohein hagadol*.) Hillel told him, only one who understands kingship is appointed king - go learn about kingship (*kehunah*)!

So, the potential convert went and studied about the laws of being a *kohein*. As he was reading the verses that discuss *kehunah* - he reached "*Veha'Zar ha'Karev Yumas*" and asked who is considered a *Zar*. (A zar "outsider" is any non-*kohein*. A zar is prohibited from doing any work of a *kohein*.)

Hillel explained, "This applies [to any non-*kohen*,] even to King David."

The future convert reasons, "Yisrael are called children of Hashem, out of His love he calls them "*Beni Vechori Yisrael*", nevertheless "*Veha'Zar ha'Karev Yumas*" applies to them - all the more so it applies to one who comes to convert with his staff and bag!

The non-Jew returned to Shamai and said, "I cannot be *Kohen Gadol* – '*Veha'Zar ha'Karev Yumas*' (you should have told me this, instead of driving me away)!"

He returned to Hillel and blessed him, for "Your

humility caused me to come under the wings of the *Shechinah* (The Divine Presence)!"

The three converts met each other; all agreed that Shamai's anger sought to deter them from converting, but Hillel's humility caused them to come under the wings of the *Shechinah* (Divine Presence). However, Rav Yisrael Salanter clarifies, "There was no flaw in Shamai's mid*d*os (character traits), he held that one must react angrily to words that belittle the honor of Torah. Hillel held that one may pardon the affront to Torah in order to ultimately bring them to convert *li*shmah (for the proper reasons). (Or Yisrael, chapter. 28.)

A rabbi and teacher must show balance in their approach in teaching students. They must know when to give a strong rebuke and when to draw them close. To do this, you must really understand the student. The sages teach us, that a teacher must guide the student according to "his way". Not every child or person can be taught in the same way. This is the problem with schools today and most psychiatrists. They expect everyone to behave the same. Therefore, we have to be taught and healed differently in our own way. How many children with ADD are considered outside the norm of society when they just require more patience from their teachers? We are all too fast to jump towards medications.

R. Levi Y. Berdichev has some wise words against strong willed, rabbi preachers. The individual who corrects other Jews by speaking of their greatness uplifts Jewish souls higher and higher. He constantly speaks of Israel's righteousness and greatness, telling how great their strength is on high. Such an individual is worthy of being a leader. This, however, is not true of one who corrects them with harsh words. (Kedushas Levi, Chukas, p. 225)

A *chassid* (religious follower) of Rebbe Menachem Mendel Schneerson once left a paper propped at the door of the Rebbe's office, expecting the Rebbe's secretary to notice it and take it in. The secretary failed to notice it, and instead the Rebbe himself stooped down to pick up the paper. The *chassid* apologized profusely for causing the Rebbe such trouble. The

Rebbe replied, "Isn't this my whole job in life-to pick up the things others have left fallen behind?" (Bringing Heaven down to Earth, p. 37)

[Rabbi Nachman] often spoke to us, warning us to bring others close to G-d. He said that we should try to speak to people as often as possible, awakening them and bringing them back to G-d. His intent was that we should even discuss mundane matters with people, allowing this to lead to words that would motivate them towards G-d. Even if you only accomplish very little, bringing about only a small step towards repentance-or even just a temporary motivation-still, this is very good.

This is all the more so when you can speak to someone again and again over a longer period. You may then be worthy of truly arousing him toward G-d and bringing him close to His worship.

There is nothing greater than this, as brought out in all our sacred texts. The Zohar thus says, "Happy is he who unifies [G-d] through the wicked... for G-d praises him in all universes." (Zohar 2:128b) (Sichos Moharan, Avodas Hashem 96)

CHAPTER 9:
Too Much Light

Every person has a certain threshold of what they are able to accomplish. When a person surpasses this threshold before its rightful time, his spiritual vessel simply breaks. This is why so many spiritual seekers seem to be at first attracted to extreme aspects of religion only to then become oppositional to all forms of religion in general.

Here is one such individual: There was a person seeking to convert, who attended a *yeshiva* in Israel. For a few years Avi Thomas studied at the Yeshiva Machon Meir. It took a while for the staff to realize that this person wasn't fit to become a Jew. They said about him, "He had a fantastic memory and was passionate about Torah knowledge. He had a very dark side as well though, and a pull towards extremism. Once, this side came out, we knew he was not worthy for *giur* [conversion] studies."

Unfortunately, that wasn't the end of the story. After being chased away due to his unstable state, he turned completely against the Jewish religion, becoming a Neo-Nazi. Thomas and his wife even had given their son the middle name of "Adolf", and owned a large number of Nazi memorabilia. His wife, it was revealed, once declared in a message to a fellow National Action member that "All Jews must be put to death."

Obviously, this is a more extreme case that isn't so common, but it reminds me also of the Jew named Yeshua (Jesus). Jewish historians placed him too in *yeshiva* in Israel where he was considered to be a troubled teen who perverted the words of the Torah. Like Thomas he was a bright and smart person. So, what went wrong?

Well it's not by chance that these souls and others got themselves lost in confusion. Hashem decreed that such events should take place and that holy light should break these vessels and shatter them. We are now to lift these sparks back into their rightful place and fight them, showing the world the truth of Judaism. Exposing to the world that Jesus was a false messiah.

There is also a lesson to be learned here. If you jump too far into Judaism, or anything in life, before you're truly ready, you are prone to failure and confusion. There is a reason why a child first crawls and only afterwards walks. It is unhealthy for them to do otherwise as growth must come slowly and at the right time.

Many people go to medical school in order to become a doctor and soon quit. They never really comprehended the self-sacrifice needed in order to work in this elite profession. The same is true with becoming a Jew. On paper or from the outside, it may appear as the perfect opportunity for you, but you must truly know yourself before sailing these waters. You don't after-all want to become another statistic of a failed conversion.

Miriam Metzinger writes, "Go for psychotherapy while converting, be honest with yourself about deep-rooted family issues to ensure you are not simply running away from problems. That way you can be 100% sincere as a convert, but still may have some unresolved baggage to deal with when taking on a new life."

Miriam makes a great point here. Make sure you really talk out your issues prior to conversion. Be sure of yourself that the difficulties of your life aren't influencing your decision. So many people feel lost in life and turn towards religion for answers. While this is a good thing, it doesn't necessarily mean that you should convert which is a lengthy process. Converting will not solve your problems.

Rabbi Yehuda HaChasid writes, "Before war breaks out between nations, Hashem looks into the future. If He sees among them a man who at some point is the future will produce an offspring that is benevolent, that man will be saved. Babylonia was destroyed by the Assyrians, as was prophesized by Jeremiah. 'We tried to cure Babylon, but she was incurable,' (Jeremiah 51:9) because no proselyte was destined to come forth from that country. But why was Nebuchadnezzar saved in the days of Sennacherib, the Assyrian King? Hashem foresaw that in the future he would rise to power and be kind to Daniel, Chananiah, Michael, and Azariah." (Sefer Chassidim, Chapter 15)

It is interesting how if someone does a Jew a favor, it is never forgotten. I remember being in school and a non-Jew came to me and said that his priest told him that everyone has to do a favor for any Jews that they know. So, he offered to me, "anything that you need tell me and I will help you." I was a bit surprised, but you see here that it makes a lot of sense. His priest was correct, it is the mission of every non-Jew to lend a helping hand to the Jewish people. Therefore, even if you change your mind about conversion or are in the process, you can't take for granted any opportunity you might have to help the Jewish people as it seals your fate for good.

Sometimes we miss some important opportunities to convert people since we are so careful not to bring in the wrong people. The Talmud says that the Jews suffered the great damage of being enslaved in Egypt because Abraham failed to give some non-Jews an opportunity to convert. (Nedarim 32a)

When our forefathers refused to accept Timna she eventually distanced herself greatly from the Jewish people, marrying Elifaz and giving birth to Amalek, who grieved the Jewish people greatly. (Sanhedrin 99b)

Still though, there must be a screening process but unfortunately, its left up to the decision of the individual rabbi you approach. Maybe he is an excellent judge of character, or maybe he has had some bad experiences in the past converting those who then became non-practicing-Jews.

Rabbi Menachem Mendel Schneerson writes, "Hormones, vitamins, chromosomes, etc., make up only a minuscule portion of the body, yet they are the most crucial elements of life. Jews are one of the smallest groups of people in the world, yet they are the most vital element of history." (Bringing Heaven down to Earth, p. 246)

Reb Shlomo Carlebach once said, "If G-d had given me two hearts, I could use one for hating and the other one for love, but since I was given only one heart, I have only room for love."

He also questioned, "Why do people hate each other? Because deep down they don't believe G-d created them. If it was clear to them that there is only one G-d and that He created them, they would love each other."

The rav also said, "Do you know why there is no peace in the world? Because the world is into force. First, they force war on each other, now they want to force peace upon each other. But it doesn't work. Peace by force isn't peace. Peace is the most non-force in the world.

"Even our biggest enemies, there were moments when they knew who we are. This story might surprise you. It is about one of the big Nazi generals who shot 400 people in Krakow at the marketplace... One person fell down before they were given an opportunity to shoot him. He was laying there pretending to be lifeless, so that they would assume he was dead. He heard the Nazi general talking. He said 'You know something? If the General wouldn't order us to hate the Jews, I would become a Jew myself.' *Gevalt* (wow).

"You know what the world is all about? They express their love in the most stupid, wrong places! I don't want to get involved too much, because it hurts too much. You know, the Pope never opened his mouth when they killed six million Jews. You know the first time he opened his mouth? When we were hanging Eichmann. He sent a letter to the Israeli government, 'Please, don't hang this man.' Really, so much love...

"Love cannot be taught. All we can hope for is that we should unlearn all the hatred. Because hatred is taught. Love is from heaven. The question is not how much you love each other. The question is how much you love each other when you hate each other."

"I want to tell you one more story," said Reb Shlomo Carlebach. "During the Six Day War, a good friend of mine, *nebech*, a tank driver. They were fighting like lions. Suddenly his tank got stuck on the way to Suez, in the middle of an Arab village, in the market place. There was no way of fixing it from the inside; he had to go out and fix it from outside. So, he tells himself, 'The moment I go out, they'll shoot me anyway. The question is, should I just die in the tank, or should I go out and be shot?' He decides, 'I better go out.' He goes out and a young Arab comes up to him and says, 'I am an engineer. Can I help you?' Maybe it was Elijah the Prophet, I don't know. My friend said to the Arab, 'Aren't you supposed to be my enemy?' He answered, 'I'll tell you. If it's a fight between Jews and Arabs, I am an Arab. But the flight is not against the Jews, the fight is against G-d. I don't fight G-d.'

"You know what is heartbreaking? Ninety percent of the world is good, ninety percent of the world doesn't want death. The problem is, they are silent. Not to be believed, right? Do you think that in Germany every German wanted to kill the Jews? They were afraid. But it happened, because they didn't say anything. Nothing.

"I have to share something with you. You know, lately I'm giving a lot of concerts in Germany. This is a really good story. This person came to me after one concert and said, 'I have to tell you something: Thirty years ago, my father died. (Obviously this was during the Second Word War.) A few minutes before he died, he said to me, I have to tell you something. I couldn't tell you this any other time, but now, before I leave this world, I have to tell you; I am so afraid to stand before G-d, because G-d will tell me, why were you silent?' She cried for three hours when she told this to me. She said, 'I want you to know, I am the daughter of a good man, but he was silent.'

"You see what it is; the hardest thing is to be a Jew. Because, on the one hand, I am so angry at the world. But anyway, on a very high, deep, deep level, I have to know it's my fault, because, I have to love them first. Because, if I wait till, they love me, it will never happen. We always have to do it first. We were the first to believe in G-d, we are the first to have to go out in the world. It takes a lot of strength.

"I have to tell you over a Torah from a black brother, a taxi driver. He said to me, 'You know something? If I could, I would become a Jew.' I said, 'I'm sure you are the best man without being a Jew, but why do you want to become a Jew?' He said, 'Because, you know, I am a black man, and I hate the white man. You Jews are persecuted for so long, and you have not learned yet how to hate.' *Gevalt*.

"I can also tell you this story as an eyewitness: If you remember, during the Yom Kippur War, the Egyptian 2nd army was completely surrounded by *Yidden* (Jews), and those Egyptians were dying from thirst and from hunger. The Egyptians soldiers were giving themselves up. Israel *mamesh* gave them food and water and everything. The craziest thing was, that even that was not enough.

"I was playing for the soldiers. I was being flown by helicopter, and every three hours, stopped at another place.

"O.K. We were singing *Am Yisrael Chai* (the nation of Israel lives). In the middle suddenly, we see nine Arab coming towards us, holding up their hands. They were dying from thirst. What was the reaction of the soldiers? It's a war, right? The first thing you do is, you tie their hands and feet, right? They were prisoners of war. What do you do with prisoners? You tie them up. What did our holy soldiers do? You know, in the desert, there is no Howard Johnson ice cream and Coca-Cola to keep himself alive. All the soldiers went to their tents and brought out all their Coca-Cola to give them something to drink.

"There was a doctor there and he started looking at the Arabs, 'Are you sick? Are you burnt from the sun?' He already began doing his doctor business. And nobody had chained them yet. I couldn't believe what I saw. Someone asked them in Arabic, 'Why are you fighting us?' One of them said, 'Because we want to kill all the Jews!'

"Imagine; I would be in the American Army and a Vietnamese prisoner of war says to an American soldier, 'We are planning to kill all the Americans.' What's he going to do with him? He is not going to kill him?

"I'll never forget it. This is the children of Abraham. The soldier who asked the Arab was 19, and the Arab boy was 17. You know what he did? He said, 'I am sorry you hate me. We could be the best of friends.' This is us *Yidden* (Jews), right? Ahhh... something else. We have different ingredients than the entire world, believe me." (Excepts from the Book, Open Your Hearts, Reb Shlomo Carlebach)

There are time periods in history where it was very dangerous to convert. One such time was after Roman law made it illegal for someone to convert to Judaism. As late as 1749 a Polish Count, Valentine Potocki, who had secretly converted to Judaism, was burned alive in the center of Vilna. Even today in Iran and some other Arab countries, Muslims who convert to another religion have been jailed and occasionally executed.

However, in democratic countries, no such danger has ever happened though one could face much anti-Semitism. Modern society is still filled with hate and anti-Semitism which is deeply rooted in far right and far leftist ideologies. Even though the church today isn't what it was in the past, it has many hidden agendas against the Jewish people. Certainly, this hate is one-sided, the Jewish people have always been known to be respectful to its neighbors even though modern media likes to paint a different story.

Thus, Rabbi Eleazar taught, "The Holy One exiled Israel among the nations, only in order that proselytes might be multiplied among them." (Pesachim 87b) It is true that there were many more converts to Judaism in diaspora Jewish communities than in the land of Israel.

So, if Rabbi Eleazar was right, many new converts came about through because of our exile. You would think that we would be more forthcoming to convert people. Well as much as Hashem loves the converts, He also doesn't want to make it simple for the non-Jews to come over. After-all, it was they who declined the Torah first on Mount Sinai.

However, by the Jewish people being exiled among the nations, they are able to come and deserve the greatest place on earth, Jerusalem and the Holy Temple. While earning this prestige, those who cast away the Torah or even the seven laws of Noah have one last chance to make their life proper. Every person must fix themselves before the coming of the Messiah.

The Talmud (Shabbos 146a) asks, "What about converts, who did not stand at Mount Sinai?" How was impurity removed from their souls that they would eventually become Jewish? Rav Ashi clarifies, "Even though they themselves were not there, their *mazalos* (stars) were there. As it says in (Deuteronomy 29:14), 'those who are standing here with us today before Hashem our G-d, and those who are not here etc.'" This teaches that even those who would only later join the Jewish nation were present in some form at the revelation at Sinai. Their presence there caused their impurity to be removed.

The sages say (Yevamos 109b): "Evil will come upon those who accept [insincere] converts," and "[Insincere] converts are as burdensome to Israel as a sore" (ibid., Tosafos). This passage emphasizes that our mistakes of both not accepting the right people for conversion and also accepting those unworthy has caused us additional suffering. That is why the entire issue of conversion has not been entirely pleasant for our people. What is even more devastating is that the Torah clearly teaches us, "You shall love the convert." (Deuteronomy 10:10) We haven't fulfilled this commandment properly and we have been punished for this grave sin. So, the reference to converts being compared many times to a sore, really is our fault. We must also take responsibility for those Jewish souls that we have pushed away from Torah by our setting a bad example. When we don't act like "The Chosen Nation," we disgrace the name of Hashem.

Sometimes the light is too much, and a holy soul is taken from us, becoming secular. Even so, one can't leave the

Jewish religion. Our sages tell us that each of us forms part of a limb of the original man, Adam. Each of us contains an important ingredient that the world needs us to share with others. Some of us have found our unique calling, while others are still in the search process. Being a Jew is so powerful that one cannot convert to another religion and lose their status as a Jew. A Jew is forever, in both worlds. We have a great responsibility to the world. We have been placed on the front lines of Hashem's army. Every one of us can make a difference just because of our Jewish *neshama*, soul. It is a thrill to share this uniqueness with one another. (My Book, Kavanos Halev, Meditations of the Heart p.37)

CHAPTER 10:
Some Positivity

You might be thinking that this writer is full of negativity. I want to be around positive energies within my conversion and life. He is against most people converting, I wonder why he is even writing this book.

So, let me be honest with you. I personally want to be responsible in aiding your conversion. If I help you to convert properly, remember all that light and sparks I spoke about earlier, I'll be partly responsible for returning this light into holiness with you. What could be greater? I'm also fulfilling the commandment to love the convert. So truly I am 100% with you. I only wish those reading this, who know that their conversion is questionable, decide to undergo a proper conversion.

I want to be the one to find the next Ruth the Moabite, who was one of the greatest converts ever. She said to Neomi, "Wherever you go, I will go. Wherever you lodge, I will lodge. Your people shall be my people, and your G-d my G-d. Where you die, I will die, and there I will be buried." Ruth went on to become the great-grandmother of King David. (Ruth 1:16-17)

Hashem has a special love for converts. So much so that the Torah says, "Dearer to G-d than all of the Israelites who stood at Mount Sinai is the convert. Had the Israelites not witnessed the lightning, thunder, and quaking mountain, and had they not heard the sounds of the shofar, they would not have accepted the Torah. But the convert, who did not see or hear any of these things, surrendered to G-d and accepted the yoke of Heaven. Can anyone be dearer to G-d than such a person?" (Tanchuma (ed. Buber), Lech Lecha 6:32)

If you take the words,

וְאָהַבְתָּ לְרֵעֲךָ כָּמוֹךָ אֲנִי יְ-ה-וָ-ה

"You shall love your neighbor as yourself. I am the L-rd." (Psalms 19:18) You come to a total of 211 in *gematria Mispar Siduri* (numerical value). This shares the word, וכגר *u'vgair*, and the convert. We are commanded to love the convert equivalently as we would someone born as a Jew. (My Book, Passages of Torah p. 115)

Hashem loves the Torah. The Talmud says that each day, Hashem Himself studies Torah. (Talmud Brachos) Whatever Hashem does, we too much emulate His actions. This is why every Jew must help the convert, orphan, and widow. We must fill our lives with kindness and giving to others. That is what Hashem does all day, He gives and sustains every living being. Not just Jews, but all of humanity must seek to emulate the fine qualities of their Creator.

Rabbi Menachem Scheerson wrote, "Purify time. Each day, find an act of kindness and beauty that belongs to that day alone." (Bringing Heaven down to Earth, p. 35)

The Torah is our manual on how to come close to Hashem and to be holy people. It was given only to the Jewish people.

I see non-Jews quoting Torah and the Talmud all the time. I love all people with all my heart, but I have to admit, there is something really missing when I read their Torah quotations. Being a Jew and knowing how holy the Torah is, I feel bad for the spiritual seeking non-Jew. They can quote the Torah all they want, but they may never truly grasp it unless they convert. Even a day before conversion, they still lack the Jewish spark in its fullness to comprehend the Torah. It's as if they understand in an exterior way but not really in an internal way. They may believe so strongly about the Torah that they feel a part of it but until the actual day of their immersion in the *mikvah*, it's not a portion of their very being. I know this might be difficult for most gentiles to accept, but I believe I can state the obvious because I know the non-Jew feels this too, subconsciously.

Sometimes the spiritual gentile will attempt to argue a point in the Torah or Kabbalah with me. They think they understand these concepts well enough. They may even quote passages better than most Jews, but the Torah isn't theirs. The knowledge they may have lacks the thousands of years that the Jewish people have used to connect and expound on its meaning. The secrets of the Torah don't belong to the gentile soul. All that can be done is to externally borrow the ideas and concepts.

If you're reading this, and you still feel you have what to argue, maybe that's the proof enough that you're supposed to become Jewish. As a born Jew, I can't put myself in your shoes. I can only express what I have learned from the sages.

Which brings me back to the question, if you are a B'nei Noach, why do you learn concepts in Judaism that serve you no purpose and that are above your observance level? It is not possible for you to enter the higher *Sefiros* and realms at this time through Kabbalistic meditations. That is just the reality. If you properly understood Kabbalah and soul roots, you would understand this. However, it's beautiful that you're seeking higher levels for yourself and yearning to give to the world. I encourage you to channel this energy rightfully and study at your souls' level. I'm not saying you're not without spiritual revelations, I'm just stating that there are limits.

Even within Judaism there are different groups that bring vital pieces to our people and serve different roles. For example, the tribe of Levy which are in charge of the Temple service and the spiritual core of our nation. Only a *Kohein* can carry out their holy tasks in the Temple. No matter how much the average Jew wishes to do this they are forbidden. Even if they become the most righteous person in the world, they will never be honored to hold the position of High Priest. Each of us has our own task to complete in this world. There is nothing wrong with the fact that our souls have different purposes. Being true to yourself is of as equal importance to *Tikkun Olam* (fixing the world) as the person across the room, who has his own spiritual task to complete himself.

However, if you do become Jewish, you're united with all other Jews as one soul. Therefore, you also become responsible for another person completing their *tikkun*. Even as a B'nei Noach, there is so much you can do to help out the Jewish people.

A follower who converted wrote me, "As to the question of what challenges and difficulties that come with the process of conversion that I would like to have addressed and see changed: For me, what I watched and experienced that was challenging to the potential converts in our program, was expectations. Everyone has them: rabbi, community, and potential convert. Those who worked through the process more smoothly, were not doormats, nor did they let expectations guide their emotions in the process. I went in to the program, empty and willing to let go of what I knew in order to relearn what I needed to know. I also found strength and respectfully challenged what did not make sense to me. This made the emotional aspect of conversion go very easily. Those, in the program I was in, who could not do so met heavy challenges and often quit. To me letting go of expectations, humility, patience, and respectful strength is key to surviving the process.

"Post *mikveh*, the struggle I met was handcrafted by Hashem for me. From there, for the next several years, I came face to face with abuse, lack of financial ethics, and more that plagues our communities.

"Suddenly, the fairytale bubble I had about Jews and Judaism was popped. Reeling in devastated shock and horror. I had to decide, 3 months post *mikveh*, would I stay, or would I go? I clung to the truth that Hashem is true, Torah is true, and people are people no matter who. I learned to find my voice and challenge what is not good. I learned to use my struggle to help others. I learned to find beautiful, good-hearted Jews and appreciate them in a way I hadn't before.

"Now, 5 1/2 years later, I am better for the deep pain and struggle I faced post *mikveh*. Knowing Hashem has a plan, carried me through those heavy waters. I don't have to have a reason for or a need to understand what He sends my way. I just am responsible for my response to the struggle.

"Instead of answering what to change in conversion programs, I can only offer one tip for thriving through that struggle pre and post *mikveh*: become *bitul* Hashem (selfless in G-d's presence). Let go of expectations and preconceived notions. Know that He will walk you through the challenges He tailor made for you. The process may be filled with heartache and struggle, but it is worth every effort to work through the process. Afterall, even a caterpillar morphing into a butterfly, faces the agony of becoming primordial soup before he can have wings and fly. He just has to succumb to and go with the process." (Devorah Miriam)

I really appreciate Devorah Miriam's struggle. Unlike all the other stories I've heard, her's seems extra special to me. She realized that the process and its difficulties were there to help her to come closer to Hashem. She remained attached to her faith through and through. No matter what, she had committed herself to something and realized that these obstacles were a part of establishing her Jewish foothold.

"Through converts and penitents, the Oneness of G-d is revealed through the very multiplicity of creation. Since they, too, come forth in order to become incorporated into His Oneness, this is most precious to G-d. Therefore, the Torah stresses that one should love and encourage the proselyte. Similarly, our sages greatly praised the spiritual levels attained by penitents, who, after having distanced themselves, strive to return to G-d." (Rabbi Noson Sternhartz, Likutei Halachos, Prika Ute'ina,4:3)

I think when the potential convert is stricken with difficulties it is because they didn't analyze their difficulties and find Hashem there.

The Baal Shem Tov says, "The Ramban writes that the power of the doer is in the deed." (Moreh Nevuchim 1:69) The creation of the universe was, "like a snail, whose garment contains it and is of it." (Bereshis Rabbah 21:5) Therefore, in every pain, there is a Holy Spark from Hashem, but it is concealed within many garments...

When a person concentrates on the fact that Hashem is also there in the pain, the garment is removed, and the pain vanishes. (Toldos Yaakov Yosef, VaYechi 39a)

CHAPTER 11:
Pretending to be Jewish

I have happened upon people over the years that were pretending or claiming to be Jewish but weren't. Sometimes I don't find out for many years after they have conversed with me dozens of times, even asking advice. As a rabbi, I am offended by being misled with this. It's as if they're trying to trick me into being their friend, and there is no reason in my eyes to do this. How can I advise a person properly who isn't honest with me? Also, if you know I would have a problem with your conversion, then let's talk about it and fix it.

I've also seen many people collecting money from the Jewish community while all pretending to be Jewish. Be honest with people and say that you're in the midst of conversion, or that you're not Jewish, but to pretend you're already Jewish isn't nice. There are so many Jewish causes that are underfunded, it's like your stealing from the Jewish people if you pretend yours is a Jewish cause. We already have Messianics doing these things. We don't need normal people doing the same. There is nothing wrong with asking the Jewish people to give you charity. In fact, it is written in the Talmud many instances where the local rabbis supported local non-Jewish charities and helped out in their communities. Honesty is the only way to build trust and respect.

You can see today that Israel offers aid to counties in need. If there is a catastrophe, Israel is one of the first to arrive on the scene. The *Hatzalah* organization helps out both Jews and non-Jews in Israel. Jewish hospitals in Israel are filled to capacity with people of all walks of life. We are a people of kindness.

This kindness is often taken for granted and abused.

Thousands of immigrants from other countries emigrated to Israel while pretending to be Jewish.

So, not only do we have to worry about assimilation, we have to be weary of some of our neighbors. It has become a big problem in Israel. Some communities that are mixed with Jews and Arab have encountered some mixed dating and relationships. Many of these relationships end up badly. A naive young lady falls in love with an Arab co-worker who charms her. They later marry, and she finds herself in an abusive relationship. She has a child and they both need to be rescued. It is very common for Arabs in Israel to beat their wives and children. It has unfortunately become so common that there are organizations that are dedicated to rescuing these girls and their children from their abusive situation. This might be the case more often when married to a Jewish girl who has no Arab family to defend her rights. These mixed marriages often lead to children who are unclear of their religious status. It can go on for many generations that someone is told they are a Jew, or not one, when in fact the opposite might be the case. It has become very difficult for rabbis to tell who is Jewish. It is even more difficult when it comes to converts when we don't know every rabbi and if he was trustworthy in performing the conversion.

We always ask people that have questionable lineage, to go through the conversion process to be sure of their status as a Jew. To some this seems offensive, but it is far less harmful than just assuming you're Jewish when you really don't know. The conversion process in these cases are usually completed more easily since there is some basis to work with.

The Lost Tribes

We are seeing more and more of this idea of the lost Jewish tribes returning to Judaism. Since the exile, dozens of Jewish tribes sought to separate themselves from normal civilization, keeping the commandments in their own way. All around the world, these small tribes have recently been discovered though we don't know which are true. It is amazing how a tribe for thousands of years could be keeping *mitzvos* in the most remote places. In most cases though, the *mitzvos* they keep have become distorted overtime due to a lack of Torah resources. When the Messiah arrives, part of the return of the exile will be the hidden tribes returning to Israel. Hashem is opening up a little glimpse of this, through the discovery of a few of these lost tribes. However, without Elijah the Prophet to guide us, we can't be sure of these tribes and their full Jewishness. At the same time, we cannot ignore them, as it is quite an unusual discovery. Something certainly is Jewish about them, but we cannot call them Jews just yet. However, we can open our hearts and find inspiration from them. We can see a glimpse of how the final exile will truly surprise us.

Our present generation which is here to greet the Messiah, is the generation that was at Mount Sinai. The Jews of today (and even the lost tribes that are returning to Israel) are all reincarnated to experience the redemption.

Rabbi Menachem Robinson wrote, "Now we are in the year 5779 which means that everything has to be completed in the next 221 years which is called the Messianic age. The return to Israel, the land producing, the final stages of Gog and Magog, the ingathering of the exile (including the 10 lost tribes), the coming of the Moshiach, the rebuilding of the third Temple, judgment day (the too late date) and the resurrection of the dead all will occur by the year 6000." (The Absolute Truth)

Pretending to be a Jew from Birth

On the other hand, we have actual converts pretending that they were born Jewish. They shouldn't have to do this. Has our welcoming committee been so bad that they have to hide their own identity? Shame on us.

Trying to look at the situation from your point of view, I can understand why you would do this. However, your conversion is a huge *kiddush* Hashem, something you should advertise to the world in order to inspire us all to serve Hashem.

114

You can see this from the story of Yisro. Hashem was so proud of His convert that He named an entire Torah *parsha* (portion) after him. He wanted to show the world the *kiddush* Hashem a convert can make. So too, you should be proud of your amazing return to the Jewish faith.

I always love encountering those converts who, with self-confidence, proclaim their marvelous journey. They inspire me, and they know that they are a light to the Jewish people.

It says, "The Torah of G-d is perfect." (Psalms 19:8) But can there be an imperfect Torah? If a non-Jew is prepared to accept the entire Torah with the exception of one law, we must not receive them as a Jew because the Torah they are ready to accept is not the perfect Torah. (Talmud Becharos 30b)

I think this is a very important message for those that did not convert in an Orthodox manner. Unless you don't believe in the oral Torah, it is impossible to take to heart these words.

If your conversion was not done in a way that you accepted the entire Torah the day of your conversion, you're simply not Jewish. You might be pretending to be a Jew, but you're not one. Do these words insult you? Well, maybe that's a good thing, so that you will do over the conversion properly.

One of the reasons people have so much trouble trusting and accepting new converts is because a large amount of them didn't convert the right way and are questionably Jewish. This makes it even harder for all of those who worked hard to convert through the proper means.

Many who convert through Orthodoxy hold onto some unhealthy habits which they bring with them into the community. This puts fears in the eyes of the Jews, thinking that maybe these influences will affect their children or others in the community.

Habits such as continuing to listen to secular music with lyrics which are inappropriate for a Jew to hear, watching television and movies are not good for one's soul. Any materialistic drives which are beyond the normal ones that other Jews have, could spread like wild fire to others in the community. It is these fears that give a bad view on new converts because all too often, some are converted before they were ready for the full Jewish commitment.

You might ask, "Why mention these bad habits when most of the Jews I know are doing these things anyway?" Well, that doesn't make it right and remember, you're a special light for our nation. You have come forward accepting upon yourself a perfect Torah. What better way to do so than to throw away all the unhealthy habits that aren't from a good Torah way right at the beginning of your conversion. It may not be easy to accept, but it's the truth.

We are told in scriptures that the person who was secular and became observant is at a very high level for making such a wonderful change in their life. But, in a certain aspect, the convert is on an even higher level, since the change is more drastic.

It is interesting to note that marrying a convert is also praiseworthy. "If a goodhearted man marries a convert who is charitable, modest, benevolent, and sweet-tempered, their children will be righteous and virtuous. It is better to marry the son or daughter of such parents than to marry the offspring of parents who are both born Jewish, but do not possess these admirable qualities, because the children of such a righteous convert will inherit their parents' splendid character traits." (Sefer Chassidim, chapter 15)

So, what do we do as religious Jews when we meet a new convert to our community who wants to become our friend? Should we not inquire about their conversion in order not to embarrass them? But what if there is a serious issue? What if they aren't properly Jewish? It is a big problem. One that I am faced constantly as a rabbi.

People often ask me for guidance about their lives. Sometimes they enquire as to what Torah material I recommend that they learn, only to find out years later that they didn't fully convert. What a waste of my time and theirs.

I think people have a responsibility to be forthright, at least when they come to a rabbi with Torah questions. This is one of the reasons, people feel uncomfortable with new converts. Nobody knows what's really going on with them. What a shame that both sides are stuck in this predicament.

Now if you were to quietly ask someone else who knows them, being careful not to speak *lashon hara*, this might be the best alternative than to be a nosey detective. But only if you truly require this information for the good of you both, otherwise, it would certainly fall into the category of *lashon hara*. Rabbi Yehuda HaChasid continues, "When speaking to a convert, a Jew should not mention the convert's former religion, speak in derogatory terms about it, or say that he is taking a dim view of it." (Sefer Chassidim, Chapter 15) In other words, you may be treading a thin line when you speak about a convert behind their back or in their presence, so think twice. You're not allowed to hurt their feelings unnecessarily. They are fragile from the suffering they had to endure in order to arrive at this point. You cannot even imagine what they have gone through.

Pretending not to be a Jew

On the other side of things, you have people pretending not to be Jewish. Reb Shlomo Carlebach was once giving a concert to a group of Buddhists. When it was over, a few of them surrounded him saying, "Hey, we didn't know Judaism was so beautiful!"

"What's your name, brother?" Shlomo asked each one as they approached. They identified themselves by their Sanskrit names, but Shlomo shook his head no, that's not what he was seeking. "Before you assumed your new name," he said gently. What was your name before that?" "Oh... Katz!" laughed one. "Schwartz!" smiled another. "Rosenbaum!" mumbled a third, all embarrassed. Obviously, they were all Jews with Jewish names. As he was leaving, one said to him shyly, "the Jews are a very spiritual people. If there were more rabbis like you around... the Swamis, Yogis, and Gurus would all be out of business!" (Holy Brother p. 164)

Let me tell you, maybe for these brothers, they were never touched by Judaism through their parents and grandparents. However, for some, their parents simply got so used to hiding their Jewish identity in order to feel safe, that they just began to forget their Jewishness. So many people have found out they were Jewish while their parents were breathing their last words on their death beds. Can you imagine finding out this way? Do you wonder if you were actually a born Jew and one of the forgotten ones?

Once Reb Shlomo Carlebach was on a flight when he noticed an unusual stewardess. An hour into the flight, he rose to stretch his legs and noticed "Kathy" praying from a *siddur*, prayer book. He approached her, "Holy Sister, you're an angel from heaven! What are you doing?" Kathy explained that even though her parents weren't Jewish, she had always been drawn to Judaism. "I have no idea where this love comes from," She told Shlomo, "but it has been so compelling in my life that I recently converted." Kathy told Shlomo that she had studied for years under the guidance of an orthodox Jewish rabbi, had undergone a thoroughly *halachic* conversion, and was now a practicing Jew. Shlomo and Kathy conversed at length, until a passenger called for her assistance and Shlomo returned to his seat.

Several minutes later, Kathy approached Reb Shlomo tentatively. "You know, since you're a rabbi, maybe you can help me with a pressing problem I have?" "It will be my honor and privilege to be of service to you, holy sister," Shlomo rejoined immediately. "Well, here's my problem," Kathy stated hesitantly. "You see, I'm in love with a Jewish man whose parents, although not religious in the slightest, strenuously object to him marrying a convert. They've been carrying on something terrible, screaming and crying and threatening to disown him should we in fact marry. We love each other very much, but he is also equally devoted to his parents, and doesn't want to cause them grief. As a result, he's terribly torn. The whole thing's incredibly ironic because I'm much more of a

Jew than his parents are! Nonetheless, I'm fearful that he's going to cave in under the pressure and call off the engagement. Can you help me?"

"I will indeed try my best to help you," Shlomo promised. "Give me the phone number of your fiancé's parents, and I'll call them as soon as I arrive at my hotel. I will do my utmost to convince them not to oppose your marriage."

When Shlomo reached the father of Kathy's fiancé, he found him hostile and unreceptive. Despite his best attempts to make the father listen to reason, Shlomo made little headway. His pleas fell on deaf ears. As Shlomo persisted, the man grew increasingly irate. Finally, he snapped, "Listen here, I'm a Holocaust survivor, and because of what G-d did to the Jews, I hate *Yiddishkeit* (Judaism), but if my son marries a *shiksa* (non-Jewish woman), I'll kill him!" Shlomo soon realized that meaningful dialogue with the father was impossible and bade him goodbye. He then reached for the phone to call Kathy and report, regretfully, on his lack of success.

It was Kathy's father, however, who answered the phone, and he too was antagonistic and contentious. He was angry at Shlomo for attempting to mediate between the two families and castigated him for his "interference". Silently absorbing the torrent of abuse, Shlomo responded with a Talmudic tale. "Now that G-d has finished creating the world, the Talmud asks, what does He do all day? The Talmud answers that G-d spends one third of His time making *shidduchim* (marriage partners). So," Shlomo said humorously, "I'm just trying to give G-d a little help in His world. Obviously, your daughter and her fiancé love each other very much. Wouldn't it be a terrible shame if they did not get married?"

Something in Shlomo's voice must have touched the man because he began to cry. "I'll tell you a secret that nobody else knows," he told Shlomo, "and until your call came, I thought I would never share it in my lifetime. My wife and I are not really Christians, we are Jews. We are in fact Holocaust survivors, and because of what G-d did to the Jews, we came to hate *Yiddishkeit* and renounced our heritage. We never officially converted, but we pretended we were Christian and raised our children as secularists. To this day, they don't know the truth about who they really are."

"But if this is the case," Shlomo responded, "and Kathy is Jewish by birth, then there is no problem. Her fiancé's father objects to her non-Jewish parentage. If you will tell her the truth, the obstacles barring the way to her *bashert* (destined one) will be removed." Kathy's father tearfully agreed, and Shlomo spent the next few hours on the phone, making a flurry of calls between two sets of parents. Finally, he arranged for them to meet in his hotel room the next day.

When the two fathers were formally introduced and rose to shake hands, they blanked in shock and recognition. A series of varying emotions-confusion, astonishment, pain and awe-fitted across their faces in rapid succession. "Herschel!" Shouted one in jubilation. "Yankel!" yelled the other in joy. To the bewilderment of everyone present, they fell into each other's arms and cried.

"We were *chavrusas* (learning partners) in *yeshiva* together before the war!" they cried out in explanation to their wives and children. "We were best friends, but I thought you were dead!" they exclaimed simultaneously.

The reunion was tremulous and tearful. Floodgates opened, and reminiscences were invoked of a long-lost era, forever gone. They spoke of their youth with sorrow, with nostalgia, and with yearning. Finally, one looked at the other and said with a crooked, funny smile. "Do you remember the fanciful pact we once made, as we dreamed about the future?" The other laughed delightedly in remembrance. "Why yes, I do! How strange, how very strange!" he murmured and turned to Kathy and her fiancé to elaborate.

"This is indeed curious, but I promise it is true. When we were *yeshiva bachurim* (boys) together, we promised we would forever be friends, and to solidify the friendship we pledged that when we would marry and have children, we would betroth them to one another. It seems that even though we forgot this pledge, G-d did not. Against all odds, you met each

120

other and fell in love. I ask you Rabbi Carlebach, how do you explain this? Is this coincidence or is this Providence?"

Reb Shlomo, who hadn't said a single word while the reunion was taking place, just leaned back in his chair and beamed.

CHAPTER 12:
Where to Study

The internet has enabled people to reach out to Jewish communities across to the globe, to show their interest in conversion. There were times where I would receive dozens of interested parties each week, via e-mail. If they were very serious, I would forward them to a local Chabad or orthodox rabbi. In all likelihood, the majority would never make it through the conversion, especially when some lived in Arabic or anti-Semitic countries. I've actually received inquiries from almost all Arabic counties which is why I hope to translate this book into Arabic and other languages so that the resources are there for those in need.

As far as people living in areas where there is an orthodox rabbi to learn from, the question then becomes, how eager is this person to properly convert? Are they willing to make serious life changes in order to correctly convert?

In many cases, people felt that they could not relocate due to their job and worry over finances. So, they continue their study mostly alone without the proper resources. Maybe you want to refer to them as a so called, "self-made-Jew"? They figure that eventually after they become Jewish, they will reevaluate where to live. As an experienced rabbi that knows what is needed for a successful conversion, this explanation doesn't really cut it for me. However, for some rabbis, they found this as an opportunity to make an entire online conversion program in order to earn a living off this group of people. I don't want to be fast to judge them, but from my experience, this is preposterous. But you know what, maybe this is the future after-all? I mean so many people really can't relocate for good reasons.

However, if you met the person of your dreams, would you not relocate anywhere in the world just to be with them? Of course, you would! So, you why won't do the same for Hashem?

Converting to Judaism is a hands-on experience. You must surround yourself with Jewish people and those practicing the traditions. It is something to learn and experience hands-on. There is no way to have a true *Shabbos* experience on your own. You must understand that becoming Jewish means that you have to change your entire life. It means self-sacrifice and making a completely fresh start. Leaving what you know and your comfort zone.

Therefore, it is very important to not only move to a Jewish community but to choose one wisely. To find a good rabbi who already has a conversion program in place and who works already with a *bais din* (Jewish court). The first thought people usually have is to send someone to a local Chabad house. Not all Chabad rabbis are the same. While some may be extraordinary in their outreach, others may not be as experienced with how to guide a potential convert. I found many obvious choices to send converts to for help, but surprisingly concluded without success. There are even major cities around the world where I know first-hand of cases where they refused to help obvious converts.

Some orthodox communities won't even hear me out when I have called them for help to convert someone because they have had such bad experiences in some parts of the world. They stumble upon people wanting to convert only to get a free ride to Israel or to escape a troubled life.

There are some communities that are known to have many converts and are therefore filled with the support needed to go through this difficult change. Going to a small town which is close knit, might make you feel as if you stand out too much as someone new and different. Others, however, could be wonderful and warm. Do your research well. It's best to visit a few times on *Shabbos* before you make your final decision.

If you think that your conversion won't involve tears

and difficulties, you're mistaken. That is why it is so important to surround yourself with good people, especially others who have already converted or who are learning just as you are.

I think one of the most important experiences that a future convert needs is *Shabbos*. It is important to spend *Shabbos* with many different Jewish families to really get a feel for this fundamental practice. While there, you can ask questions about keeping *kosher* and other things that you're learning. *Shabbos* is such an important part of your studies that you need to surround yourself with both Jewish families and a synagogue weekly. There is no way you can get this from online study or from a book. It's simply not the same. I recommend that every week you eat your *Shabbos* meals at different families and build yourself a support group of Jewish friends. Ask the rabbi who is teaching you if you can join his family regularly for *Shabbos* meals. This is truly the best way.

As far as possible concerns about moving and leaving what you are familiar with, in order to join a Jewish community, do you really think that Hashem will abandon you for doing the right thing? Not only is it important to prove to those helping you convert that you're willing to make sacrifices, but to show Hashem, Who is watching to see your level of faith in Him.

Binyamin Yisrael wrote me, "I know of a Caribbean guy in my community who lived in a shed to complete his conversion."

Over the years, I have known many converts who never fully assimilated into the Jewish community. Instead, they would schedule occasional visits for *Shabbos* to complete their conversion. This continued even after they converted. Some remained living in the same home as their non-Jewish relatives. They only suffered from doing this. It is like they were still living both lives and never really put the non-Jewish one behind them. They suffered from severe loneliness as they never had the community support around them. They never found a *shidduch* because people didn't know them well as they weren't regularly in the community.

On the other hand, some who did move to a Jewish community, chose the wrong ones. They picked small communities with few people inside them. They too, never got the support they needed and suffered after their conversion.

Many of these people were still holding onto their past life. Others are so attached to their physical possessions that they could never simply leave. Some had the book knowledge to convert, but their emotions weren't balanced enough to integrate into the Jewish society.

An anonymous person wrote me, "I have full access to resources, and I am living by Judaism many years, but because of lack of money I cannot convert to Judaism in my local area - London, e.g. Masorti (Conservative Movement) provide wide range of conversion for £3,500.00 which is unaffordable to me. Another orthodox group require tutorials for money. I do not want tutorials because I am living by Judaism and maybe know better materials than the provided tutors. Conclusion is obvious - only rich people can be converted and Judaism is for rich only, particularly in London. I am Jew in my heart anyway, and I am looking for a Hashem acceptance only! Not some created by humans' rules?"

This person has obviously encountered some difficulty trying to convert. Having not met him nor heard the other side of this story, it's difficult to fully judge the situation. However, it's sad to hear that he has concluded that he knows more than most Jewish tutors, and he feels that he is more capable of finding Hashem himself than through the rabbis. You know, it's true, many non-Jews who grew up in very religious Christian homes are quite knowledgeable in Bible studies but that doesn't mean they understand them in a Torah way. They can sometimes out quote many rabbis but that only proves that they have a good memory. Not that they understand the material and live it. That is why I am not such a huge fan of debating with non-Jews, you can take many words from the Bible easily out of context and it's an endless battle to put them all back into place.

I personally haven't charged for Jewish lessons, but I

can understand why some might. Just like when you take a college course or go to technological school, you have to pay for the teacher's time and patience. Then again, quite honestly, if someone is really serious about conversion, I don't see how you have the right to turn them away because of their lack of funds. Nowhere in the Torah does it say that the Jewish people should charge for conversion. The *bais din* (Jewish courts) that I know of in America charge nominal fees for conversion. There is a saying that if something is completely free, a person won't appreciate it as much. Maybe this is also something to consider. Should you find that the teachers you have turned to in order to help your conversion seem to be more interested in your money than your soul, it's a pretty good sign that you should find a new teacher.

Someone once came to me and told me that they were paying hundreds of dollars a month to study conversion online. In fact, they were told by this so-called "online rabbi" that they should not go to their local Chabad to study. I immediately instructed them to stop their study, and I contacted the local community rabbi for them. There instructor should have done the same instead of promoting online study when unnecessary.

You have to pray very hard to find the perfect rabbi who will embrace you. Let me share with you a story of one rabbi who saw the good inside everyone.

Once, Reb Shlomo Carlebach was taking his usual Friday night *Shabbos* walk along Manhattan's West End Avenue, when he was attacked at gunpoint. "Give me all your money or I'll shoot you on the spot!" screamed the mugger, waving his gun. Undaunted by the gun, Shlomo smiles good-naturedly at the man, and patiently explained, "Holy brother! I feel so sorry for you that you have to do this. I would really like to help you out, but I'm so sorry, it's *Shabbos* and I don't keep money on me. If you will please come tomorrow night to my synagogue after the *Shabbos* is over, I will be glad to give you whatever you need." After hearing Shlomo's gentle words, the mugger lowered the gun and let him go. Something about Shlomo must have convinced this mugger that Shlomo would not turn him in because *motzei Shabbos*, after *Shabbos* sundown, the mugger kept the appointment and showed up at the *shul*. Shlomo gave him some cash and the man vanished, never to be seen again. (Holy Brother p. 147)

Besides from finding a nurturing rabbi, at some early stage of your conversion, you will have to decide to start separating yourself from all negativity. You can't become holy without some separation. The world has become all too filled with negative vibes.

Rabbi Pinchas Koretzer once told a man not to live in a small town. This person's thoughts were not strong enough for him to be constantly able to fortify himself to attach himself to G-d. He therefore had to be careful not to live among gentiles. (Midrash Pinchas 25)

If you were to ask me, which is better, to live among positive minded gentiles or negative minded Jews, I would find that a difficult call. I'd just suggest that you search for more positive Jews to be around. Don't settle for anything less. It is better to be alone than to be around constant negativity. I bless you that you should find positive people in your life.

CHAPTER 13:
Living in Israel

There are some that desire to convert and move to Israel. To do this, one must have proper conversion papers from a recognized *bais din*, Jewish court that is approved in Israel. It is something you must look into before you just assume it will be easy.

The Orthodox-controlled Chief Rabbinate in Israel does not recognize non-Orthodox conversions, so you won't be able to marry an Israeli Jew, should you convert through Conservative or Reform. Orthodox converts must prove their Jewishness, and the Chief Rabbinate has been known to look suspiciously even on some rabbis affiliated with the Rabbinical Council of America. If someone converts outside of the Torah's laws, they are a convert outside of the Torah's laws, but the Torah law itself will not consider them a convert to Judaism.

Living in Israel also has its challengers. Instead of just one lifestyle change, you're talking about a huge leap into new waters. Living in the Middle East comes with a new set of challenges. Peoples' mentalities and attitudes are different. Don't assume you're just going to make *aliyah* and suddenly make a lot of new friends. It could take you years before you become fluent enough in Hebrew and even then, most of your friends will probably not be Israeli. Israelis think and live differently than the English-speaking culture you grew up in.

However, it can be a wonderful experience to live in the holiest place in the world. Some converts assume, since I have already given up all my old family and friends, I might as well just go all the way and move to Israel. This may be true, but it may not be for everyone. It would be good to spend many months in Israel to see first-hand if you can adjust to the new culture. It will not only be a change to live as a Jew, but there will be other lifestyle changes, far more than you realize.

On the other hand, life here in Israel can be spent much more simply with priorities given to family life and culture. Not having to compete with your neighbors for the fanciest house or car, will save you a lot. Even the manner of dress here is simpler. We are always behind in the latest fashions. Bills are easier to deal with and pay. However, over the last few years, the cost of living in Israel has sadly risen. Buying an apartment can be stiff and set you back a fortune. Rent prices and the cost of living seems to be higher than the average salary. That is why it is so important to donate to poor families in Israel which often consist of large families.

Often English speakers find it more worthwhile to setup an online job oversees than to receive the lesser salaries Israelis earn. It is very wise to setup an online job before you come if you are able to. If you do so, you could live very comfortably in Israel instead of needing to save up for everything. After a few years in Israel, you really find that you don't need to live such a materialistic lifestyle as you once did. You can do with far less and in fact, you might lose your desire for fancy items completely over time. The holy land is quite purifying in all aspects.

Sometimes, we learn the hard way, as to what is truly important. Israel really teaches us this first hand. Even amongst many non-religious Israelis, there is still a certain underline faith in Hashem. It is quite common for the simple Israeli taxi driver with no *kippah* to encourage you about G-d and Torah. The holy land is filled with magic, I must tell you. For a country that has such a problem with terrorism, Jerusalem is actually one of the safest cities in the world to live in.

Some people desire to do their entire conversion in Israel. This is not just a hop over trip, convert in a few weeks and return home. It takes years of committing to study in a *yeshiva* or seminary in order to convert. Israelis are fully aware that rushing conversions isn't a good practice. They will want you to stay in their school and make a few years commitment to study. I think this is a wonderful idea as then you will completely surround yourself with Judaism. However, when you have an entire family that will convert with you, this may become a bit more complicated. You will need enough money set aside for years of study without working since you can't legally work here without a permit (unless it's on the black market), or you will need to get a working visa of sorts. Also, to stay here, you will need a student's visa that can be extended periodically through the school. It is something you will need to really research to see if its within your means and right for you at this time. One thing I can tell you, it is one of the most unique gifts from Hashem to live here. However, everyone has their calling and purpose. It could be that your soul needs to rectify things in your local city first.

Reb Shlomo Carlebach told, "There is a *sefer* [holy book] from the Kotsker Rebbe's grandson. He says there something unbelievable. When G-d gave the land to Abraham, G-d says to Abraham, 'Go to the land, which I will show you.' Here the Kotsker Rebbe's grandson says something awesome: There is no *mitzvah* in the world which is as unclear as the *mitzvah* of living in Israel because G-d says to Abraham, 'Go to the land which I will show you.' That means that you only can go to Israel when G-d shows it to you.

"Israel is given to the people who G-d calls. G-d is calling them, but until you hear it, you don't feel at home. You need a special privilege to hear it.

"You know, sometimes you see a *Yid* (Jew) with a *shtreimel* (fur hat) in Borough Park, right? He doesn't go to Israel, but you will see a *Yiddele* (Jew) who eats shrimp on *Yom Kippur*, and he is crazy about Israel. That means, *mamish* G-d told him, 'Go'. I mean, that he heard it. You need a special privilege to hear it. You know, basically there should be a big sign in Lod Airport, 'If you heard from G-d, then you can come.'

"I met this stewardess on Northwest Airlines, and she

told me, 'What's wrong with you Jews? G-d gave you the land, why don't you go there? If I ever convert, and I am thinking about it, I convert in the morning, and that same night I move to Israel. Because if I am a Jew, I don't want to live anywhere else.'"

There is a certain gathering of the exiles that you slowly see taking place with so many Jews returning to Israel. However, there are sparks that still must be uplifted around the world. Some rabbis think that if all the Jews around the world would hop on planes and come to Israel, the Messiah would instantly come, but that sounds too easy to me. There is still much work to be done. Therefore, some Jews must stay behind and elevate and uplift the nations. Someone like myself, so involved in Jewish outreach online, it doesn't necessarily matter if I live in Jerusalem or America. With technology and the writing of my books, I can spread the light of Hashem everywhere. That is, if you will also help me in my ventures. One candle can light up another but when people come together, that one candle can become a torch and light up the world.

CHAPTER 14:
How Long Does It Take?

Most conversions are rushed. People want to convert as soon as possible, even thinking they can convert within a few months. Rabbis may be eager to get another convert under their resume. However, there is nothing healthy about a rushed conversion. Does a child learn to walk before they can crawl? Does someone become a professional ballplayer before first going through the amateur rankings?

The Evil Urge will not entice you not to study Torah at all. It knows that you definitely will not listen to that. When you do not study at all, you will be considered an ignoramus, and you will not have any status among your fellows.

The Evil Urge therefore tries to entice you into not learning things that bring you to fear of Heaven. It will prevent you from studying books of rebuke (*mussar*) and the Codes of Jewish Law (Shulchan Aruch), so that you will not know the proper way to behave. At the same time, the Evil Urge will tempt you constantly to study Talmud with all commentaries. (Tzava'as HaRivash p. 232)

In most cases, I find that converts waste valuable time studying Jewish classic works that have little relevance on their main task right now, studying what applies to their conversion. While I am not saying other study isn't also helpful, it certainly should not be the focal point. The same seems to be true with many B'nei Noach. They feel that since they are not under the personal guidance of a rabbi, that they can pick and choose anything in Judaism that satisfies their thirst, even if it has no practical application. They might even care less that the Torah was given to the Jewish people and have personally accepted it as a gift from G-d without His blessing. While I could claim that this is disrespectful in some way, to literally take the Torah as your own without any of its responsibilities, I think it will fall on deaf ears. It reminds me of my strongly religious Christian photography professor. He told me that each week, his church chooses their own leader from the congregation. Why should they have an ordained leader to tell them what to do. This way, their church belongs to them and they each have the opportunity to lead it and interpret the Bible as they choose.

Once, I attended a synagogue in Israel that asked me to help them with funding. I asked them why they don't have a rabbi. I told them that people want to support a shul that has some leadership. He responded, "We talked it over with our congregants and we don't want the pressure of having to agree with one rabbi's objectives. We would rather each choose our own way and have visiting rabbis from time to time speak." I tried to explain to him that this isn't how Judaism works. Leadership is good. You can't have a synagogue without a rabbi.

My point is, G-d doesn't want you to do whatever you want. Yes, the Torah is meant to be enjoyable, but every person must learn inside their level. The Torah isn't an encyclopedia to just memorize. If you don't believe that the Torah is being misused and distorted, just Google the word Kabbalah. You will see an enormous amount of misinformation. This information comes from people who not only studied beyond their level but who dared to teach a Torah they had not received from G-d. There are even some Jews who unfortunately twist the holy Torah in order to profit from it financially.

Frank Siciliano recalls about his conversion, "You have to change a lot, and you want to get it changed in a relatively short amount of time," he said. "I put the cart before the horse many a time. Patience was probably the hardest part of the whole thing. I wanted to get it all done quickly, and that's just not smart. Going from praying once a week for 45 minutes at church to praying every day was not easy to schedule at first."

The day you convert, you become responsible to keep

all of the commandments. If you convert before you're already keeping the commandments properly, then you will not only start out your new life as a sinner, but you will hurt the Jewish people, delaying the Messiah's arrival. You will feel depressed and sad knowing the countless mistakes you are making. Pushing yourself to fix this, you will take upon yourself a lot of new commandments at once, feeling overwhelmed and tired. There will simply be too much responsibility upon your shoulders, and you will give up, adding yourself to the countless Jews who don't follow the traditions. Also, your conversion will now become a question to yourself and others. Was this a *kosher* conversion after-all? Were you truly keeping *Shabbos, kosherus* and foundational commandments at the time you immersed in the *mikvah*?

Within Judaism, you don't pick and choose which commandments are easy that you would like to keep or which ones you find difficult to just pass over. I have people coming to me telling me that they converted and photos of them show that they have no *kippah* on. They do study Torah, but they enjoy spirituality. Online they seem to identify themselves as Jewish, but I guess they never moved to a proper Jewish community, and they have no intensions of outwardly showing this Jewishness. They may even have two online profiles, a Jewish one and a secular one. Maybe they are embarrassed since they haven't fully separated from their old lifestyle and friends? Just this alone seems to draw into question their Jewishness. I'm troubled though, as a rabbi, I wonder why they would go through years of study just to do something half-way. How does this bring them and their family contentment? They have truly put a thorn in the side of the Jewish people causing us more harm than good. Why didn't they just stay B'nei Noach? What rabbi is responsible for converting a family before they were ready?

I always say, if you're going to do something in life, do it 100% because otherwise, you're not really doing it. If you're going to commit to something, if you make a major decision, see it through all the way. That way, at the end of the day, you know you gave all your best.

A person wrote me, "Although it is possible to convert, it's not for everyone. I'm thankful it is so hard. It weeds out those who are serious and those looking for a quick fix."

The most important part of learning Torah and converting is enjoying the adventure. Rabbi Menachem Robinson writes, "If you are not enjoying what you are doing, you are doing it incorrectly. Hashem wants this to be a very joyous experience." (The Absolute Truth)

CHAPTER 15:
Who Approves Your Conversion?

At first your rabbi is going to weigh in as to when he feels you're ready to convert. He should not only look at what you have accomplished with your studies, but also look to see if you're emotionally ready for this huge change. Hopefully he is a good judge of character.

Most prominent rabbis have connections with a Jewish *bais din*. A small *bais din* can be made up of just three qualified rabbis who studied extra laws permitting them to judge cases. This is a huge responsibility as from the time of Moses, each Jewish community had their own judges whose job was to bring peace in the community.

Prior to your conversion, your rabbi will connect with the *bais din* to introduce the idea of your conversion. When approved, they will help with the final steps like the immersion in the *mikvah*, testing your knowledge of basic concepts and circumcision if necessary. Since the idea of *bais din* is new to you, I can understand why it might seem scary, however, they are just there to help. Some *batei din* have a greater reputation than others. You should go to one that is well recognized and accepted. If you're planning on making *aliyah* to Israel one day, make sure the *bais din* is recognized in Israel.

Gary Buchanan once wrote me, "For me it's like a man prospecting for a motorcycle club. You need to go through the hard testing of character and knowing what it costs." Gary brings up a good point here. Your rabbi and *bais din* will be observing you to see if you are really committed to becoming Jewish in all its particulars. This is because they are responsible for your soul after the conversion.

I think this is one of the reasons many conversions are so difficult for the people afterwards. I don't know if their rabbi, or those who helped to convert them, understood that they have now become responsible for this new soul for the rest of their life.

Usually what happens is the new convert and their teachers usually loose contact. They often go their separate ways. The people who were their new family are now far from them, and they are on their own in the huge world of Jews.

In some cases, I have had converts call me asking that I help them get into *yeshiva*. My first question is, who converted you, and why are they not involved now in your life? The answer I usually receive is that the rabbi doesn't seem to help them so much anymore, and they are on their own. The next thing I know, I'm on the phone lecturing a well-known rabbi on how he is responsible for this soul he converted. The call doesn't always end well, as all I hear are excuses as to why this person is no longer worthy of the effort. I have responded once, twice, "why do I have to clean up your mess." I then use some of my contacts to help the convert out in the correct way. This doesn't hold up well since everything starts to lead back to the rabbi who converted them, so I just try to do my best. If you ask me, if you're not willing to follow up on your converts, don't make them. It is much harder for someone like me, as an outsider, to get involved.

This is a two-way street though. It isn't just the rabbi's responsibility to follow up but also the convert. Many times, while ridding themselves of their old lifestyle, the convert also unties themselves from anyone who knows that they converted. They choose to break all prior ties before their conversion. The whole process looking back was traumatic, stressful, and they just want to put it behind them.

They might even start to rethink if the rabbi was truly correct on how he guided them. Maybe they feel like they were misled much of the time. There seems to be a lot of people to blame for a very stressful conversion. "Why aren't I married?"

they might ask. Whatever the reason, the rabbi or the *bais din* are old news, they have moved on to greener pastures. I have found that people who convert and keep contact with their first Jewish family, are more content. It is very healthy to keep this relationship going. I don't know if they truly appreciate how much effort it took for these people to guide them. Those seeking conversion were coming from a world completely unknown and secular to them, yet they opened their home and families to them. If that isn't true sacrifice and love, I don't know what is. So, don't just move on, leaving these good people behind.

CHAPTER 16:
Keeping Kosher

Why Keep *Kosher*?

To explain this in the simplest way, Jews must keep *kosher* because Hashem commanded us to keep *kosher*. The word *kosher* actually means "proper or fit". In other words, anything that is done correctly according to Jewish law makes it *kosher*. That means not just food, but it pertains to a Torah, the prayer shawl, other things we do or wear, etc.

A wonderful source of information about Judaism is from Aish HaTorah, a *yeshiva* in Jerusalem with offices and programs worldwide. Here is a very good write-up giving us concise reasons for keeping *kosher* (this only is covering the dietary law concept of *kosher*).

Moral Lessons: We are taught to be sensitive to others' feelings – even to the feelings of animals. A mother and her young are forbidden to be slaughtered on the same day, and of course, "don't cook a kid (goat) in its mother's milk." (Deuteronomy 14:21)

The Torah prohibits cruelty to animals. We must not remove the limb of an animal while it is still alive. When we slaughter an animal, it must be done with the least amount of pain possible; there is a special knife that is so sharp that even the slightest nick in the blade renders it impermissible. This prevents pain to the animal. (I will cover this subject separately, with the proof that ritual slaughter is totally painless and even of great benefit to the animal. You don't believe it? Stay tuned).

Another moral lesson is that the animals, and all food as well, affect our character traits. This is why all kosher animals

139

are herbivores, and we are not allowed to eat birds of prey.

National Reasons: the Jewish people have a mission of *tikkun olam*, repairing the world or "healing the world". A special diet reminds us of our mission and keeps us together as a people to fulfill it. We also have a prohibition against eating meals and drinking wine with gentiles. When one eats a meal with others it brings a levity to one's demeanor and may lower the guard of Jews. Through this restriction it helps to alleviate things like inter-marriage and inter mingling which will cause a Jew to stumble with regard to keeping the commandments and staying holy.

Keeping *kosher* is also a reminder of gratitude to the Almighty for taking the Jewish people out of Egypt, and a symbol of the holy covenant. (see Leviticus 11:45-47)

Mystical: The Torah calls the Jews a "holy people" and prescribes a holy diet (see Deut. 14:2-4). You are what you eat. *Kosher* is G-d's diet for spirituality. Jewish mysticism teaches that non-*kosher* food blocks the spiritual potential of the soul because these animals are spiritually impure.

Kosher animals, properly slaughtered and prepared, have "sparks of holiness" (according to the Kabbalah) which are incorporated in our being.

Discipline: If a person can be disciplined in what and when he eats, it follows that he can be disciplined in other areas of life as well. *Kasherus* (keeping *kosher* dietary laws) requires that one must wait after eating meat before eating milk products, and we may not eat certain animals or combinations of foods. (Even when you're hungry!) All of this instills self-discipline.

I guarantee that Hashem knows exactly what is best for us. Non-*kosher* food to the soul of a Jew is like poison to the body. As we would never consider eating arsenic laced food or serving it to our family or friends why would we serve poisonous food to our soul? Physical death can ruin your day. Spiritual death lasts forever. If you think this is an exaggeration, I highly suggest you don't test it. You will not know the truth until a time that is called "too late".

When it says you are what you eat, we actually pick up the personality and characteristics of the food we eat. It is totally a spiritual concept that from the soul of the food we are eating, our soul is affected. As an example, a cow is a very docile animal. A pig is a slob and even a very deceptive animal. He has one of the two physical characteristics of a *kosher* animal (split hooves) but hides the fact that he is not *kosher* (he doesn't chew his cud). This trait of being deceptive, by displaying his paws and pretending that he is a *kosher* animal, is transferred to the eater (not a favorable personality trait). We don't eat birds of prey because we should not be people of prey and aggressive.

What confidence do I have in this information? Total, since it comes from Hashem, but let me give you a more miraculous confidence measure (in case you require more help in believing). It says in the Torah that we can eat from any animal that has two physical traits. The animal must have split hooves and chew its cud. That is really all the information that is needed, but yet the Torah continues to tell us a warning. It says, "beware there are four animals that have one sign but not the other." (Leviticus 11:4-8)

The camel, for being a ruminant (ruminants are mammals that are able to acquire nutrients from plant-based food by fermenting it in a specialized stomach prior to digestion, principally through bacterial actions), without their hooves being divided.

The hyrax, for being a ruminant without cloven hooves. The Hebrew term for this animal - שפן *shaphan* - has been translated by older English versions of the bible as *coney*; the existence of the hyrax wasn't known to early English translators. The *coney* was an exclusively European animal, not present in Canaan, while the *shaphan* was described by the Book of Proverbs as living on rocks (like the hyrax, but unlike the *coney*).

The hare, for being a ruminant without cloven hooves.

The pig, for having cloven hooves without being a ruminant.

This sounds like very good information to help us identify *kosher* versus non-*kosher* animals. Is this implying that whoever wrote the Torah knew every animal that ever was, is and will be? Is the writer of the Torah willing to lose total credibility if there are other animals not mentioned here that can be found with only one sign? You bet!!! The miraculous answer is there has never been another animal found in the 3327 years since Hashem gave Moses the Torah on Mount Sinai (there are variations of the above animals, but they are still in the same family). I guess the credibility goes completely to the One Who happens to know every animal throughout history (since He created all of them).

Let's go one step further. It says in the Torah that the requirements for a fish to be kosher is that it must have scales and fins. Once again, that is enough information to recognize a kosher fish, but in the oral Torah (the Talmud) it warns us that there are fish that have fins, but not scales and they are not kosher. It goes on to let us know that there aren't fish that have scales but no fins. Is this implying that whoever wrote the oral Torah knew every fish in every sea, lake and river that ever was, is and will be? Is the writer of the oral Torah willing to lose total credibility if there are fish that can be found that have scales but no fins? You bet, again!!!

Simple conclusion is that we know beyond a shadow of a doubt Who dictated the written and oral Torah, letter by letter, to Moses. If the miraculous information here testifies to the total credibility of the writing of the Torah, the information that is in the Torah is also totally credible. There are, by the way, an infinite number of miraculous bits of information in all of Jewish scriptures – this was only one example.

Don't mess with the commandments especially since they are for our own good. They are the tools to succeed in this world and for eternity. You owe it to yourself and your loved ones. Just be aware that for a Jew to observe the dietary laws is not just a cute tradition handed down for thousands of years, they are vital instructions for survival. There are dire consequences for not doing what Hashem asks of us and they last for all eternity. Once again, we should never argue with success. When you treat this information as a gift from Heaven to help us be happy, we should say "thank you" rather than ask "do we have to?" (Written by my father-in-law, Menachem Ben Reuven z"l, in his book "The Absolute Truth")

Our sages teach us that a person should not say, "I do not like the flesh of swine." Rather, he should say, "I like it, but what shall I do when my Father in Heaven has forbidden it?" (Sifra, Rashi on Leviticus 20:26, Shemonah Perakim #6)

The [Mezricher Maggid] said that it is speaking only of a person who has never sinned. One who has sinned, however, must be repulsed by all evil. In order that he not fall, he must say, "I do not like it." (Rabbi Schneur Zalman, Likkutey Torah, Ve'es Chanan 9d)

The Bal HaTanya emphasizes this a lot in the Tanya. He says that it isn't enough to dislike evil, you must absolutely hate the idea of sinning. The mere thought of a sin should disgust you so much that you would not even remotely consider it. If you are open to it in anyway, then you keep the desire open giving the Evil Inclination an opportunity to tempt you.

In the Zohar, we do find the concept of eating with relation to G-d. King Solomon also said [in G-d's name], "I have eaten My honeycomb with My honey, [I have drunk My wine with My milk,] eat O friends, drink, yes drink abundantly, O My beloved." (Song of Songs 5:1)

We also find that G-d calls Israel, "My sister, my friend." (Song of Songs 5:2) The Midrash interprets "My friend" to mean, "the one who sustains Me." (Shir HaShirim Rabbah)

It is important to note that Hashem considers Israel His friend. He wants us to be satisfied and to be amongst Him. Rabbi Mann of Tzfat zt"l once mentioned to me, "If you want to connect to someone and make them happy, feed them delicious food." Should you find that your spouse or children are upset with you, give them something sweet to eat and it will calm their anger and sadness.

Food has a unique way of connecting us to Hashem. Without eating we would perish after a few days. Through eating, we have faith. We have faith that Hashem will provide us with our needs. We recognize that we are blessed to have this meal that sustains us.

That's why it's so hard to understand why someone would not appreciate *kosherus* enough to eat *kosher* to the highest of standards. One of the mistakes many newcomers make is not putting enough emphasis on *kosherus*. This extends not only for the food you keep in your house but also that which you eat outside your home is of equal importance.

Keeping *kosher* really is a fundamental part of being holy. A person might attempt to feel spirituality (like *Shabbos*), but unless they have eaten *kosher* food that day, the soul will not be purified enough to fully accept holiness. It is like filling a barrel with wine yet there are pinholes throughout the barrel. The wine simply pours out and is not retained. A person could do everything right in his Judaism, but if he doesn't eat *kosher*, everything will be lacking. Only with a pure vessel can a person truly experience G-dliness.

That is why if someone converted to Judaism and at the time was not fully keeping *kosher*, their conversion is meaningless. So fundamental is keeping 100% *kosher* that without it, you simply can't become a vehicle for holiness.

When G-d said, "Let the earth bring forth grass... and fruit trees," (Genesis 1:11) and "Let the earth bring forth living creatures," (Ibid. 1:24) it was that statement itself that gave existence to the particular thing that is its innermost Life Force.

When a person eats a fruit or other food, they recite a blessing over it with feeling, saying, "Blessed are You, O G-d." As soon as they mention G-d's Name, they awaken the Life Force through which that fruit was created [and is sustained]. Everything was created through G-d Name, and therefore, since, "each thing finds its own kind," [the Life Force associated with G-d Name] is aroused.

It is this [Life Force] that is the food of the soul. This,

however, is only true of permissible, *kosher* food. It is this that G-d commanded us to elevate from the physical to the spiritual.

[The reason why only Israel says such blessings] can be understood through an example:

A king once lost a valuable jewel from his signet ring. Standing before the king at the time were many of his servants, ministers, generals, and officials. The king did not want any of them to search for the stone. Instead, he told his only beloved son to search and find the lost jewel so that he would be able to return it to his father.

Even though the king fully trusted that each of his ministers and servants would return the stone if he found it, he still did not want them to look for it. He wanted to give the merit of finding it to his beloved son.

Besides that, the king gave many hints to his son as to where to find the lost jewel. He had lost it on purpose and knew where it was. The only reason he did so was to give his son the merit of finding it. The king himself also had immense pride and delight from his son, and he proclaimed, "See! No one in the world was able to find the jewel except my son!"

The parallel is this: At the very beginning, the world was created in order that Holy Sparks could be separated through the people Israel. Our sages therefore comment on the verse, "In the beginning G-d created the heaven and the earth." (Genesis 1:11) "In the beginning-for the sake of Israel, who are called 'the beginning'." (VaYikra Rabbah 36:4) For in eating permissible *kosher* food [and reciting a blessing over it] it is they who separate [these sparks]. (Keter Shem Tov 194)

I'm fully aware that often B'nei Noach desire to eat *kosher* thinking it will bring delight to the Creator. However, G-d didn't command them this, He desires that Israel keeps *kosher*, and this is what brings Him delight. He did, however, give you this commandment. "The Prohibition of eating meat taken from an animal while it is still alive." (Genesis 9:4) G-d obviously cares very much for the pain of His creatures, and He wants you to likewise respect His Creations.

If you could inspire even one Jew to keep *kosher*, this would bring G-d great delight. Should you soon become Jewish and keep *kosher* properly, you will see how truly great it is for your soul. For a Jew, without keeping *kosher*, you can't even begin to serve G-d. That is why it is one of the main trainings a convert learns.

Whenever you eat, wear, or make use of anything, you have pleasure from the Life Force in that thing. Without this spiritual essence, that thing could not exist. This essence contains the holy Sparks that are related to the root of your soul.

When you make use of a utensil or eat a particular food, even for the sake of your body, you rectify its Sparks. They are rectified when you use the strength derived from the food, clothing or other things to serve Hashem.

When you finish rectifying all the Sparks in something that relates to the root of your soul, Hashem sometimes takes it away and gives it to someone else. This is because Sparks still remain in this thing, which relate to another root.

When people eat, drink and utilize things, their main goal is to absorb the sparks that exist in each thing. You must take care of your possessions because of the sparks that exist in them. It is most important to consider these Sparks. (Tzava'as HaRivash p. 231)

For the rest of the nations, eating is just to sustain the body. However, for the Jew, eating takes on an all new meaning. Eating becomes entirely spiritual.

The soul is carved out of a holy place and should constantly burn to return to its Source. In order that it not be annihilated out of existence, it was surrounded by a material body, so that it should also be involved in physical things, such as eating, drinking and business. As a result, it is not constantly involved in worshiping Hashem [and does not become nullified in His Essence].

For this reason, the Emanations (*Sefiros*) have levels of both Greatness and Smallness. [The level of Greatness corresponds to their] "return". [These levels also have their parallel in man.]

When a person has a constant enjoyment, it becomes part of his nature, and is no longer an enjoyment.

Man must therefore go up and down in his worship of Hashem. He is then able to sustain the enjoyment which is the main purpose of worshiping Hashem. (Keter Shem Tov 121)

Everything is seen with its spiritual reality foremost. However, it takes years of purifying one's mind and heart, to attain this.

Rabbi Moshe Vorshiver, of blessed memory, questioned the holy Rabbi Eleazar of Koznitz, "How did you merit becoming a *chassidic rebbe*?" He answered in four parts: "First, I never prayed for myself alone without including others. Second, from everything that I saw I learned a lesson. Third, in everything that I saw, I did not see it physically, but its spiritual essence."

To demonstrate this latter point, he told of how he once traveled with a young scholar to Warsaw. When he went to be with the *chassidim*, the other young man remained behind at the inn. Upon returning there later, he inquired where the young man, his traveling companion, was. They told him, "He's sitting over there." However, to the rabbi, he simply appeared to be a goose. He glanced at him more closely and realized that, indeed, it was he. Then he asked him, "What have you been doing?" He responded, "I've been enjoying myself eating – I had a delicious meal of goose."

There was also a fourth thing that the rabbi said. He never put his faith, nor trust, in anyone other than Hashem alone. (My book, The Pathways of the Righteous p. 21)

How can you listen to the Evil Urge and sin? Rather, you should learn from the Evil Urge, which constantly does Hashem's will. (Toldos Yaakov Yosef, Pikudei 78b)

The Ari, of blessed memory, speaks of the separation [and elevation] of the Holy Sparks. These Sparks fell at the time when G-d, "built universes and destroyed them."

One must separate these Sparks and elevate them [step by step], from the inanimate to the domain of plants, animals, and humans. These Holy Sparks are in the husks [of evil] and must be elevated. This is the goal of the observance of the Torah and commandments. (See Etz Chaim, Sha'ar Man U'mad)

This is also the concept of eating. It is known that each Spark, even the inanimate and plant domains... has a complete structure, with 248 limbs and 365 vessels. As long as it is in these lower domains, it is imprisoned. In this state, it cannot stretch out its hands and feet or speak. This is alluded to in the verse, "Its head is on its knees, on its insides." (Exodus 12:9, referring to the paschal lamb)

When, with these good thoughts and intentions, a person elevates the Holy Spark from the plant realm to the animal and human, he liberates it. There is no redemption of captives greater than this. (Baba Basra 8a)

[Here is an example]. If a king's son was in prison, and someone came along and worked to free him, his reward would be without bounds. (Ibid.)

All this is judged and calculated on high. It is written, "He makes an end to darkness." (Job 28:3) It is thus determined how long the Spark will remain imprisoned, when it will be liberated, and through whom. (Ben Poras Yosef 74b; Keser Shem Tov 53)

The disciples of Rabbi Yisrael Baal Shem Tov were once sitting together and discussing the main thing with which the leaders of the generation must concern themselves.

Some said that the most important thing was to oversee *kasherus*. They should be concerned that the slaughters (*shochetim*) and butchers should be G-d-fearing, and that everything else should be in order. This is most important, since non-*kosher* food plugs up the heart [spiritually]. (Talmud Yoma 39a)

Others said that the rules regarding carrying on the *Shabbos* were the most important. We are taught that the laws of the *Shabbos* are "like mountains hanging from hairs." (Talmud Chagigah 1:8) The laws are very important and the prohibition very severe.

Still, others said that the main thing was the *mikvah*, and it should be carefully supervised to see that it is built according to the law, without any question. [To have intercourse with one's wife, who has not immersed in a proper *mikvah,* is one of the worst possible sins, and this has a very strong adverse effect at conception.] If the foundation of man's structure [at conception] is not proper, it is very difficult for him to overcome evil.

The Baal Shem Tov replied, "A similar argument has been brought up in the Academy on High (*Mesifta DeRakia*) They said that all three opinions were correct. These are the foundations of the world." (Birkas Avraham, Ve'es Chanan)

It is no wonder that these *mitzvos* are emphasized as fundamental in the conversion process. They are clearly very important. If they are not kept properly, then all the other *mitzvos* are affected.

CHAPTER 17:
Jewish Ritual Slaughter

Now, hopefully, I convinced you that keeping *kosher* is not just an old Jewish tradition, but a commandment that is a matter of survival. One might bring up a very controversial subject that we find in the news these days, Jewish ritual slaughter. After all, the Torah is supposed to be very humane in the way all of Hashem's creations are treated; how come there is so much debate worldwide about this method of slaughter?

A quick description. Jewish ritual slaughter, called *shechita*, involves using a very sharp knife to cut the carotid artery at the neck of the animal. It is interesting that this method is totally painless for the animal. How so? The blood flowing in the carotid artery is directly connected to the blood flowing in the vertebral artery at the back of the neck to the brain. This causes immediate cessation of blood to the brain and instantly renders the animal unconscious. There is absolutely no pain felt by the animal because the unconsciousness occurs immediately (actually within a second or two, but definitely before the brain gets a signal of pain).

What is fascinating is that this connection of the carotid artery directly to the brain only exists in all animals that are *kosher* animals. Hashem designed *kosher* animals to allow a totally painless slaughter. A non-*kosher* animal's carotid artery is not connected directly to the brain, meaning it would not fall unconscious and would experience great pain. This method was commanded by Hashem and given to the Jewish people 3327 years ago at Mount Sinai. It is the only humane method of animal slaughter in the world. It is only out of complete ignorance and the growing Jew-hatred in the world that it has become a topic of debate in recent years.

A definite requirement in the process is that the knife, by Jewish law, must be an extremely sharp, smooth blade with no nicks. This along with the very quick forward and reverse motion ensures the animal's total lack of pain. There have been testimonials from surgeons that perform emergency medical treatment, that a quick, sharp cut using a sharp knife is essentially painless. You may have noticed that when you cut yourself, it is generally when the blood starts to flow that the pain is felt, usually a couple of seconds after. The most reassuring proof is that the animal does not complain as with other methods of slaughter which result in obvious outburst of animal crying. If the procedure is done improperly causing pain, the animal is declared not *kosher*.

Non-*kosher* methods of slaughter on the other hand undoubtedly cause pain to animals. Very often they use numbing techniques such as an electric shock, which supposedly prevents any feelings of pain. It actually fries the animal's brain, and definitely causes unnecessary suffering. Another method is a bullet to the head which surely causes suffering. This can be even worse when delivered inaccurately, whether due to poor aim or an unexpected movement of the animal's head. Clubbing animals is also a very inhumane and extremely painful slaughter. There is no doubt that the only method used in the world today that provides sensitivity and compassion to the animal is the Jewish ritual slaughter.

There is yet another very interesting difference between *kosher* and non-*kosher* animals. A study conducted years ago demonstrated that horses, dogs, and other animals resist being brought into slaughterhouses because they sense their approaching death. They become agitated and may even kick and fight until they are killed. In *kosher* slaughterhouses, this phenomenon is almost non-existent. For example, lambs present at the slaughter of other lambs do not show signs of fear. A calf allowed to roam freely during a period of *shechita* did not attempt to run away, even though the door of the slaughterhouse remained wide open. In addition, cud chewing animals will cease to ruminate when they are under stress. However, cows in a Jewish slaughterhouse may even sit and ruminate while members of their own species are being slaughtered around them. All this indicates that not only do *kosher* animals not suffer during ritual slaughter; they do not even experience emotional discomfort before the act and have absolutely no sense of their impending deaths.

Still, since there is always the possibility that one of such animals will be more sensitive than the others, Jewish law forbids killing an animal in the presence of another, in order to prevent even the slightest chance of suffering to the one remaining alive.

Meat slaughtered for consumption must be kept hygienic and safe throughout the duration of its storage, both for health reason – to avoid food poisoning – and economic ones – so as not to needlessly waste food. In general, the higher the quality of the meat and the fresher that it can be kept, the less the need for discarding of the meat, ensuring that fewer animals need to be slaughtered. According to some researchers, *shechita* ensures higher quality meat than other forms of slaughter. Shooting, for example, leaves an excess of blood in the carcass, due to the time lag between death and the bleeding of the carcass. This causes the meat to spoil faster. In other non-*halachic* methods of slaughter, the situation is even worse. (With regard to this topic, we should note the *halachic* requirement to salt meat after slaughter in order to extract the remaining blood. This act is derived from the prohibition against consuming blood – primarily a spiritual commandment, which has obvious health benefits as well.)

There are other very big advantages to the animal being killed according to Jewish law that are obscure and would not even be considered. Animal sacrifice has some additional characteristics that are virtually unknown but very beneficial to the animal.

(Written by my father-in-law, Menachem Ben Reuven z"l)

Chapter 18:
Shabbos

Of all the topics that I could talk about, *Shabbos*, or the Sabbath as you English speakers say, is definitely the most misunderstood concept. In fact, most people reading this have no idea what *Shabbos* is. You may ask: "Isn't *Shabbos* the day of rest, a day that we can't do any work, a day that we are totally restricted from everything?" If you ask that question, then you are exactly the individual who needs to be educated about *Shabbos*.

First of all, you should know that *Shabbos* is the greatest gift from Hashem to the Jewish people. Even though we are commanded to remember and observe the *Shabbos*, there is nothing more enjoyable than *Shabbos* if you do it correctly. We see that the seven Noachide laws given to the non-Jews do not include *Shabbos*. The fact that the Muslims celebrate their Sabbath on Friday and the Christians on Sunday is no accident – it is from Hashem. Saturday, the day that Hashem finished the creation of everything and rested was designated as a gift for the Jews of the world to join Hashem.

The word used in the Torah to tell us it is not a day of work is מְלָאכָה which translates to craftsmanship or created effort. When the Israelites were building the portable Tabernacle in the desert, they performed 39 different skillful activities in making the Tabernacle. When Hashem told us to rest on the *Shabbos*, He referred to those 39 activities. That is why turning on a light switch is forbidden but moving furniture around to accommodate guests is permitted. Moving furniture is not a creative activity of the 39 but building or destroying is. Modern interpretation shows that completing an electrical circuit is a building activity and should be avoided (there are other authorities that equate closing an electric circuit with starting a fire, or at least the idea of a transfer of energy which is one of the 39 activities to avoid). If you don't see switching on the light as a building process, then you have proven that you have not studied the interpretation of the great rabbis who are giving you the word of Hashem. Even if something is a precautionary effort just to make sure, you are showing Hashem your willingness to adhere to His will, and you will come out in His favor. Never forget that this is the world of testing, and Hashem notes everything you do to serve Him. Anyone who doesn't agree with the great rabbis is not serving Hashem, since we know that Hashem is the One Who put the guidance into the minds of the rabbis and made them the authorities to help us.

Let us talk about the more spiritual purpose of *Shabbos*. We are actually given an extra soul on *Shabbos* to bring us to a much higher spiritual level. Until you experience this higher level of spirituality, my words mean nothing. It's like trying to describe a new taste that you have not experienced. The only way for you to appreciate that taste is to put the food in your mouth and enjoy. The extra soul has a very hidden advantage. We are told that with this extra soul you can get a taste of paradise right here on earth. Once again, that is meaningless unless you try it.

Shabbos has another great advantage that is also very hidden. We start on Sunday to prepare for *Shabbos*. The entire week is buying the food, preparing the food, getting clean clothes ready, setting up timers, setting heating and air conditioning controls, inviting guests (or accepting invitations), cleaning the house, preparing words of Torah to be talked about at the *Shabbos* table, etc. This is the greatest lesson in preparing us for the real world – the World to Come. I have mentioned that this world is only a place of testing and perfecting ourselves. When we prepare for *Shabbos*, we must not overlook one thing. Why? Because whatever you did to set up for *Shabbos* is what you have available when it starts. We cannot fix things that we forgot to do in preparing for *Shabbos*. You have to live with your effort and what you completed Sunday through Friday. You cannot fix something in this world, in this life after you leave it. What you did in this world is what you are blessed with or stuck with forever. What a valuable lesson for setting up your eternity is practicing with *Shabbos*.

Another example that might be more familiar. After months of counting the days, vacation time is here. You are planning a trip about which you are very excited. The preparation was nerve-racking, but it is all done, and you and the family are ready to go, go, go. You have your plane tickets, you packed everything (hopefully), you made hotel reservations, ground transportation arrangements, someone to take in the mail, feed the dog, make the house look lived in (to trick the burglars), travelers checks, traveler's insurance, etc. Whatever you did is what you will live with. If you forgot to make a reservation and the hotel is full; if you forgot to take the money that was sitting on the dining room table and the bank account is drained, if you forgot to... You got the idea. A successful, enjoyable vacation (or holiday if that's what you call it) is all based on the preparation before the event. Just like *Shabbos*, just like life – now and forever, you must prepare and make sure everything, and I do mean everything, is done properly. Fortunately, Hashem gave us a roadmap to get us totally prepared. It is up to us NOW to use it.

What about the restrictions of *Shabbos*? The fact is, it is just the opposite. During the week we are slaves to this materialistic world. Whatever we need we have to do something to accomplish it. On *Shabbos*, everything is done. The food is cooked the house is ready even the lights and heating system is set and doesn't even need our effort. Best of all, the world goes away. There is nothing more emotionally upsetting than looking at the news and seeing all the chaos and turmoil happening in the world.

In the 1960's, there was a Broadway show entitled

"Stop the World, I Want to Get Off." The world sometimes becomes so tense that we think the same. On *Shabbos* the world goes away. My bills go away, my work problems go away. I love it. I am not restricted; I am free from the craziness of this world and the harsh requirements to live on it. I know *Shabbos* ends and the world comes back. That is when I start my countdown to the next *Shabbos*.

I should mention that *Shabbos* is the best day of the week to study Torah. The phone doesn't ring, no traffic outside (cars and buses are not allowed to operate in my hometown on *Shabbos*). There are many study groups and lectures available. Many friends are available with which to study, who are not always available during the week. No school, so the children and grandchildren get extra attention and study – they love it also. Of course, dad and grandpa also get extra attention.

A little caveat: There is one vehicle that travels through the streets in our city – he is the *Shabbos* goy. A non-Jewish fellow who will fix, adjust, change, turn on, turn off, you name it. He knows the *halachos* as well as, if not better than, most of my neighbors, and therefore will get the job done without any worry of a *Shabbos* violation.

What is one of the most special days of the secular year in America? Thanksgiving. Why? It is a beautiful day of being with your loved ones, eating scrumptious food, relaxing and above all the world seems to go away. Jews have 52 Thanksgiving celebrations a year (more if you include holidays, WOW). A big difference is that the family is truly together – in the same room, not in different worlds, watching football.

We are forced to pay attention to each other on *Shabbos*. On *Shabbos*, we sing, we talk Torah, we laugh, we smile, we have a very, very good time. The best part is we have become so close a family that when the grandchildren came into our lives, the *Shabbos* was the ticket to love and happiness with the new generation. A very hidden pleasure in the Jewish community is a much lesser generation gap.

If anyone tells you they don't enjoy *Shabbos*, they are doing it wrong. There is nothing like it in the secular world. I thank Hashem so much for this gift, a gift that is so great, you have to experience it to understand what I am saying. My words mean nothing, your experiencing *Shabbos* means everything, and you get good marks on your final report card from Hashem, the gift Giver. (Written by my father-in-law, Menachem Ben Reuven z"l)

Our sages teach us, "Whoever keeps the *Shabbos* according to its laws is forgiven all his sins, even if he commits idolatry like the generation of Enosh." (Shabbos 118b)

As you can see, there is a direct connection between observing the *Shabbos* and rectifying the sin of idolatry. Most new converts at some point lacked faith in their life. Their commitment to *Shabbos* therefore rectifies this. That is why *Shabbos* is one of the most important commitments of someone converting.

A king's son was once kidnapped and held in the worst possible captivity. Many years passed while he waited and hoped that someone would come along and ransom him. So that he could return to his father.

After a very long time, this prince finally received a letter from his father. The letter told him not to give up hope, and not to forget the ways of the king while among the "wolves of the night". It reminded him that the king's hand is stretched out and ready to bring him back to his father's house in any way possible, whether through war or through peace.

The king's son rejoiced very greatly, but this was a secret note, and it was impossible for him to celebrate it openly. He therefore invited all the townspeople to the tavern and treated them to drinks. All the people then rejoiced in their wine, with a very physical joy. At the same time, the son was rejoicing because of his father's letter.

This is precisely the reason why we have a commandment to enjoy the *Shabbos* (*oneg Shabbos*). (Isaiah 58:13, Shabbos 118a)

We take the physical body and allow it to enjoy food and drink. The righteous individual can then rejoice in a very different delight, for this soul is bound to G-d all that day.

(Toledos Yaakov Yosef, Kedoshim 98b)

The *Shabbos* is a special secret between the Jewish people and G-d. While the world suffers with confusions and stress, we take a day off to just rejoice in holiness.

It is written, "Remember the *Shabbos* day and keep it holy." (Exodus 20:8) We have to keep the holy *Shabbos* even if we don't understand the reason for it. Just because G-d commanded us, is enough.

The *Shabbos* is like a great wedding. People are dancing and celebrating with boundless joy and delight. You are standing outside and looking in. You put on your best clothing and quickly run to the wedding, wanting to join the festivity, but you need great merit even to look in through a narrow crevice. (Sichos Haran 254)

This is similar to the B'nei Noach that attempts to add to their required commandments. They recognize that there is definitely something special about keeping *Shabbos*. They begin to slowly observe this day in their own way. However, they are only able to look through a little peephole to see what *Shabbos* truly is. Without the Jewish *neshamah*, soul, *Shabbos* simply isn't a gift from G-d.

If a person has never worn nice clothing, and then puts on beautiful clothes, they have immense joy. The same is true with *Shabbos*. Even if you don't understand it, if you prepare for it and make both a physical and spiritual change in yourself, you must feel something.

This, I believe, is the feeling someone who isn't Jewish feels during *Shabbos*. They recognize the extraordinary joy of the day and from this alone they begin to feel something. It is like they are yearning for holiness and to be connected. But still, the only way to truly feel the *Shabbos* is to receive it as a gift from G-d.

"The *Shabbos* is therefore called a 'good gift'. When one keeps the *Shabbos* according to all its laws, this 'gift' consists of forgiveness for all his sins." (Kedushas Levi, Ki Sisa p.161)

It is written, "Keep the *Shabbos* to make it holy." (Deuteronomy 5:12) This can be understood in the following manner.

G-d created the universe with two concepts, Direct Light and Reflected Light. The concept of Direct Light is that which is distributed to the universes, each one according to its particular aspect. The universe of angels thus does not perceive any more than is appropriate to that world, and the physical universe also only perceives what is appropriate. The Light, which can be perceived by the universes, is called Direct Light.

The concept of Reflected Light is that which remains later. It does not enter the worlds, since they cannot accept its brilliance. This light, therefore, returns to the Infinite Essence and constricts itself.

The concept of the Constriction (*Tzimtzum*) involves this Reflected Light. It cannot be grasped by anything that was brought into existence or created, for even the highest angels cannot perceive this light.

Israel, the holy nation, however, is higher than all the universes, higher even than the highest angels. They can therefore attach themselves to concepts that are not otherwise accessible and perceive them.

It is written [that G-d grants forgiveness], "to the remainder of His heritage." (Micah 7:18) Our sages' comment that this refers to, "those who make themselves like a 'remainder.'"

The holy Rabbi Dov Ber [the Mezricher Maggid] said that this refers to those who sanctify themselves greatly with the holiness of G-d. The root of this concept of holiness also alludes to the above-mentioned place of Constriction, which is the place that cannot be perceived.

Israel, however, sanctify themselves with respect through permissible things. They separate themselves from the physical, and from frivolous delights, which are the concepts that exist in this world [and are visible in it].

They attach themselves only to things which are above the physical world, and which therefore cannot be perceived. This only relates to the Infinite Essence.

[They therefore bind themselves to] the "remainder" of the Light that is distributed to the universes, which the worlds cannot tolerate. This Light then returns to the Infinite Essence. The concept of the "remainder" is that of the Reflected Light, as discussed above.

The nations of the world only receive concepts that exist within the worlds. This is alluded to by the six days of creation in which the worlds were completed and is therefore the concept of distribution. They do not have any conception beyond that which exists within the universes, since they cannot perceive anything beyond this.

Israel, on the other hand, can perceive concepts that are even high than the universes. They therefore keep the *Shabbos*, which alludes to the Constriction. This also alludes to the concept of holiness, which refers to the separation from this physical world. (See Reshis Chochmah, Sha'ar Hakedusha 1) This is an attachment to that which is higher than this world, and which cannot be perceived. This is the meaning of the verse, "Keep the *Shabbos* and make it holy." (Kedushas Levi, Yisro p.137)

You see to truly experience *Shabbos*, you have to first purify your soul by separating from the mundane. A person can't just walk into *Shabbos* and expect to be on the level to experience its light. The light of *Shabbos* is special and reserved for the Jewish people. The *Shabbos* is simply too high to be perceived by regular souls. Even for a Jew who has just one *Shabbos* experience in their life, it may not be enough for them to appreciate its splendor because *Shabbos* is above the physical world which may be the only world they have previously chosen to be familiar with. It takes a lot of prayer and a lot of hard work to be a vessel for the light of *Shabbos*.

It is imperative that the future convert exert much effort into learning about *Shabbos*. They must get used to observing the *Shabbos* and being around Jews during *Shabbos*. Don't make the mistake of being left out of this important day.

Reb Shlomo Carlebach taught, "You know, when you love someone very much, you cannot imagine the world existing without them, right? You know what it is to believe in G-d? It doesn't mean that I believe there is one G-d. I believe that Reagan was the president of the United States. Not the same, right? To believe in G-d means I cannot imagine that there is a world without G-d. I can't bear it. You know, to keep *Shabbos* is not simply that when *Shabbos* comes, I close my store. Do you know what, for us Jews, it means to keep *Shabbos*? It's that I cannot even imagine to be Sunday without *Shabbos*, right? I cannot even imagine Monday without *Shabbos*. I cannot be without *Shabbos*, right?"

CHAPTER 19:
Being Embarrassed to be a Convert

One of the reasons many converts distance themselves from the rabbi and community they started out with is in order to hide their identity as a convert. This is because, as much as we are to welcome the convert into our Jewish congregations, we seem to sometimes look down upon them. This is sad and completely against the Torah, but it is still the reality on the street. Some converts prefer that others will think of them as *ba'alei teshuvah* (Jews who return to orthodoxy) instead of a convert. They don't want to feel like a second-class citizen.

This is very unfortunate because to me a convert to Judaism is inspirational. I love them with all my heart, and I feel like they give off a tremendous light to our nation. To publicize that you're a convert is to make a great *kiddush* Hashem.

However, I can't judge those who wish to hide their identity. There is nothing wrong in *halacha* for them to do this, except when it comes to looking to marry. It is truly sad, and it must be very difficult emotionally to not be yourself in public because of the fear of *lashon hara*, slander.

Miriam wrote me, "Imagine a girl who is crying into her hands. You go to her and ask, 'What's wrong?' She is sobbing at this point, and she looks at you with tears in her eyes, and asks, 'Is it true that I'm not a Jew? I did everything to get here, and someone had to tell me I'm not a Jew after I poured my heart out to *Hakadosh Boruch Hu*...because I didn't go to the right people. I didn't convert to get people's approval.

The only approval I need is from Hashem Himself. And He is the only judge in the end.' Now do you understand why people are uncomfortable saying that they are converts? I am that girl." Miriam Esther

In Miriam's situation, it wasn't that she didn't convert through orthodox channels, it was that even though she did, people many times face critics who second guess your conversion. Are all these people self-proclaimed experts on conversion? Is it their business to involve themselves? They don't do this to born-Jews in the community. So, when do they have permission to involve themselves so intricately in people's lives?

There are many situations in which people convert a bit too prematurely and therefore, like even *ba'alai teshuva*, they have to take a step back even after becoming religious, just to put their emotional affairs in place. This doesn't mean that they aren't Jewish. Even born Jews go through challenging times and have to reevaluate their religiosity at times. It seems like when a convert goes through this, it really draws the attention of everyone. It's like the Jews are looking on to see if this convert will last or just become another statistic. Instead of looking on, lend an ear my friends! Converts are allowed to be human also. They are seeking friends and family.

The greatness of the Holy One, blessed be He, is primarily revealed when the non-Jewish nations, too, come to know that there is a Divine Authority. As the Zohar states: When the idolatrous priest Yisro decided to serve G-d and declared, "Now I know that G-d is greater than all powers," the Divine name was glorified and exalted from every aspect. (Zohar II, Yisro, 69a, citing Exodus 18:11) (Rabbi Nachman of Breslav, Likutei Moharan I, 10:1)

This is the reason is that Yisro was a priest of all the idolatrous religions in Midian. This put him deep into the netherworlds of idolatry and paganism, but when he said, "Now I know that G-d is greater than all gods..." he thereby proclaimed G-d from His exalted level down to the lowest level!

163

Therefore, if you can, follow the direction of Yisro and publicize your conversion to spread the greatness of Hashem. Maybe there will be a few haters but overall, your declaration will honor the Holy One blessed be He, whom you have changed your entire life for.

Jenn, a second-generation Chinese-Canadian, converted to Judaism four years ago through the conservative movement. She and her Jewish husband visited a number of *shuls* before finding one where they felt they belonged.

"I obviously don't look Jewish. It was difficult at times," she said. "Going to certain *shuls*, sometimes people would whisper."

Some people who spotted her playing with someone else's children, have on occasion assumed she was their nanny. "That hit me hard," she said.

But both her husband's and her own family were supportive of her conversion, which was easier than she had anticipated.

Today, with her little girls enrolled in a Hebrew-speaking daycare and Jewish after-school programs, she feels part of the community. "We're surrounding ourselves with the right people, and we're very comfortable," she says. (Lita Sarick, for CJN post)

In this case, as an orthodox Jew, if Jenn visited one of our orthodox shuls, she would certainly feel out of place. She might think that it is her ethnic background, but really, it's not that. Most orthodox shuls today find people of diverse backgrounds a fresh part of the flavor of their community. Rumors of her not being Jewish according to orthodoxy would be the reason everyone is questioning why she is there. Now, it's not the way of orthodoxy to throw anyone out of the congregation for this reason but the rabbi and others would want to enquire as to what went wrong with her conversion to see if there was any way to correct it. In most cases however, the conservative convert isn't interested in any real commitment to following the full Jewish law. If they had

wanted the full Jewish experience, they would probably have
gone to the orthodox rabbi to complete their conversion. But
maybe not, maybe this is the first time Jenn realizes that not
everyone accepts quick conservative conversions. Let's, hope
she goes back to the drawing board instead of just finding a
conservative or reform congregation that will accept her for
whatever parts Judaism she decides to keep. I only wish
someone would have told her the importance of observing
Shabbos and keeping *kosher*. They probably didn't even ask her
any questions or insist she immersed in the *mikvah* first. Who
knows? With Conservative or Reform in our day, anything
could have happened. They probably didn't care if she accepts
the *Shabbos* in anyway, as long as she likes the Jewish people,
she would be welcome. The idea of *tikkun olam* doesn't exist to
them.

In a similar case, Aliza Hausman writes, "Why does
everyone stare at me in *shul*? My hair is furrier, fuzzier and a
foot taller than everyone else's. Even among 'my people' in the
Dominican Republic, I am considered rather pale; but in a
crowd of *Ashkenazi* Jews, people tend to see my measly tan as
exotic. My skin color, my hair texture and my facial features all
betray my desire to blend in. I only wish I could tell all the
gawkers outright that, just two years ago, I was a non-practicing
Catholic."

Someone replied to her, "It's better to laugh than cry.
Face this with strength and humor...Besides, the rabbis said it
wasn't easy being a Jew!"

Another convert writes, "As a half-white, half-black
convert myself, I found myself avoiding the synagogue or large
gatherings."

Aliza Hausman brings us some words of comfort into
her situation, "Someday, we will get to a place as a people when
we realize that Jews come in all shapes and colors and always
have and always will. Not because of conversion, adoption,
intermarriage, mixed marriages but because we have been the
ultimate world travelers in times of strife and in times of need.
We should celebrate that diversity and own it, not stifle it or

question it or pretend it separates us in any way. It just makes us cooler and worldlier because Jews ARE everywhere, even in the most remote places imaginable, and have the most amazing customs worldwide that celebrate that diversity daily."

This was just a small glimpse at life after conversion for some. It really can be challenging to feel like you fit in. For some it really becomes heartbreaking. They set their expectations so high that we as a Jewish people fail them once they converted. That is why this book on conversion is so important to read before deciding to convert. We give you the good, the bad and the ugly side of it all hoping that if your prepared for it, you will coast through the system and not have any of these trials others might have faced. No, it's not easy transforming into a new lifestyle with new types of people but it sure is worth it. That is, if you feel it's your calling.

While you might feel a bit embarrassed to be a convert there are plenty of Jews that felt embarrassed to practice Judaism in public. They hid their *yarmulke* (skull caps), tucked in their *tzitzis* (four cornered garment), and eventually, even their inner being felt less Jewish until they stopped practicing altogether.

Let me tell you a story which hopefully will remind you of how proud you should be every moment that you can practice Judaism. Maybe then, you might decide to shout to the world how happy you are that you converted.

In the 70's, when Communism in the Soviet Union started to dissipate, Jews found the opportunity to once again practice their religion in public, but most didn't even own a *kippah* or Jewish paraphernalia. So, there were many collections that took place and rabbis would visit Russia to hand out as many Jewish items as they could.

On his first visit, Reb Shlomo smuggled in *siddurim* (prayer books), Hebrew books, *yarmulkes*, *tefillin* and other religious items. The Russian Jewish activists with whom he met accepted them gratefully, and within a few short days, all the religious materials he had brought along with him were gone. On this last day in Moscow, Reb Shlomo was packing and preparing to depart for the airport, when he heard a timid knock on his hotel door. A young boy stood on the threshold and whispered urgently, "Please can I come in?" Inside the room, the boy turned to Reb Shlomo and said, "I hear that you are distributing *tefillin* and *yarmulkes*. I came to get set for myself."

Shlomo looked at the boy mournfully and said very gently, "My holy child, I am so sorry, but I have given them all away. There is nothing left." Instantly, the boy threw himself on Shlomo's bed and began to cry wildly. "Holy Brother!" Shlomo sat down next to the boy, putting his arm around him. "Why are you crying so hard?"

"Next week is my *bar mitzvah*. I have been secretly studying the Jewish texts with some other boys my age, and although my knowledge is limited, I know enough to know that on one's *bar mitzvah* day, one is instructed to don *tefillin* the first time. There's no place in Russia where one can obtain them, and I only heard today that you were distributing them. As soon as I heard about you, I rushed here immediately. I want so badly to fulfil this *mitzvah*. You were my only hope. I can't bear the disappointment!" And the young boy began to cry again. Thoughtfully, Shlomo looked at the boy, turned to his suitcase, and took out his own personal pair of *tefillin* and handed them to him.

"My holy father, blessed be his memory," said Shlomo, "gave me this pair of *tefillin* when I was *bar mitzvahed*. They have very deep, sentimental value for me. I'm not attached to my possessions, and in fact own very little in my life. From the *tefillin*, however, one of my last links to my deceased father, I thought I would never part. But if it means so much to you to have *tefillin* on your *bar mitzvah*, then I will gladly give you mine." The young boy, unaware in his naivety of the enormity of Shlomo's sacrifice, took the *tefillin* happily and murmured his thanks. As he was about to leave, he turned towards Shlomo once again and in a plaintive tone asked, "But what about a *yarmulke*? Shouldn't I wear a *yarmulke* at last on my *bar mitzvah* day?"

"My holy child, I am so sorry, but I gave away all the *yarmulkes* too," answered Reb Shlomo. As the boy's eyes began to well up with tears, Shlomo hastily took off his own *yarmulke* and handed it to him. "It would be my privilege and honor if you would please take mine." The boy took the *yarmulke*, kissed Shlomo's hand, and left.

Shlomo Carlebach had never walked anywhere in the world without a *yarmulke*, but on that day, he departed from his first visit to Russia, he left bareheaded. Later that morning, on a connecting flight to Israel, he saw a group of Jewish men *davening* (praying) in the aisles, and he asked one if he could borrow his *tefillin* when he was finished using them. "Listen, Reb Shlomo," said the man with a derisive laugh. "I think that before you worry about *tefillin*, you should first concern yourself with the *yarmulke* that's missing from your head!"

"Oh, my holy brother," said Shlomo gently to the man. "If only you knew the story behind the missing *tefillin* and if only you knew the story behind the missing *yarmulke*. If only you knew..."

So, my friend, if you understood how beautiful it is that you converted in order to perform *mitzvos*, it wouldn't matter to you what anyone thinks. If you understood the sacrifice the Jewish people made throughout generations to publicize their observance, you would proudly scream it in the streets of the world, that you found G-d. Don't let a few detective Jews deter you, be yourself and be proud. There were so many Jews who wished they could have screamed in the streets their pride, but they had to go into hiding to perform the *mitzvos* or face execution. In our times when we can practice our observance in public and not be prosecuted, let us embrace this. Embrace the added holiness you have brought to your new family, the Jewish people and happily share it with the world.

CHAPTER 20:
Why Don't we Take in More People?

Someone asked me, "I have so many sincere proselyte-to-be friends. On the other sad hand, a number of Jews being apostates. With Muslims multiplying by the day, does conversion have to be really hard, still for them?"

This is a great question. You would think that due to being one of the largest minorities in the world, we would actually seek more people to convert, maybe even ease up the process so that more people would apply. However, this is not the will of Hashem. Better to have ten strong lions than one-hundred sheep. We want our converts to be strong in their convictions. People who are truly devoted to the Torah without shortcuts.

Philip Voerding writes me, "It makes sense that an enquirer from the Noachide Laws should add some Torah *mitzvos* as time goes on, as some rabbis have written. If one learns Torah, keeps the *mitzvos* and find they can do it with joy, then perhaps it's time to consider conversion. If one is still a B'nei Noach, and they find they can't keep the *mitzvos*, no harm is done. This person can still keep the Noachide Laws and whatever other *mitzvos* they were able to keep joyfully. My humble opinion."

Philip brings up some good points here, I would not encourage B'nei Noach to take on the rest of the *mitzvos* unless they were very serious about converting. I think it's important to stay within the areas of our soul root. I find it very uncomfortable as a Jew when I see non-Jews wearing *tzitzis* and *kippahs*. Some keeping *Shabbos* and *kosher* without any real intent in converting. However, if they were very serious about converting, it sounds like an interesting plan, but they should begin slowly. Also, you must understand that if it was Hashem's Will to give more *mitzvos* to the *B'nei Noach*, He would have done so. So, I think it's really important to choose wisely which path you want to take and stick to that one pathway. Then, in that chosen path, be the best you can be!

The Torah teaches us not to go after making converts. This is a consequence of their distance from holiness. This principle is also reflected by the tradition that when a non-Jew comes to convert, they are initially discouraged (Yevamos 47a).

"Many waters cannot quench love..." (Shir Hashirim 8:7) The Midrash Rabba explains, "The Holy One, Blessed be He, says, 'If all the nations were to come to My people and offer them all their silver and gold in exchange for just one word of Torah, My people would refuse them.'"

However, the ENTIRE PURPOSE of this initial discouragement is only to STRENGTHEN their resolve and DRAW them closer by testing them. For if after everything, they will say, "I know that I am unworthy." That is, they recognize their distance from holiness, then they are immediately accepted. (Rabbi Noson, Likutei Halachos, Shilu'ach HaKan 5:17)

Rebbe Nachman teaches (Likutey Moharan I, 17:6-7), when blemished faith begins its return to its source, anything that is attached to it will also be returned and elevated to that source! This will also explain our sages' teaching (Kiddushin 70b), "*Gerim* are as difficult for the Jewish Nation as *sapachas* (a type of leprosy)."

The obvious question then is: are our sages trying to draw in *gerim* and make them feel comfortable, or are they intending to reject them? It is true, many times they bring with them their non-Jewish lifestyles. However, within time, when the *gerim* remain steadfast in their new-found faith, they eventually bring about greater revelations of G-d in this world.

Rabbi Avraham the Ger explains, the main reason why

gerim are considered "difficult" is really a simple one. When one completes their *geirus*, their acceptance of Torah and *mitzvos* are so absolute and unbending that they put to shame the Jew who may not be so demanding of them self in observance! This slackening of the Jew's faith and devotions is compared to idolatry which arouses G-d's anger and leads to harsh decrees. (See Deuteronomy 11:16-17) By extension, this means that the contribution of converts to the nation is one of mitigating G-d's [harsh] decrees, because once they pass the initial period of "difficulty" and become integrated into the community, their faith shines and illumines all the worlds and fills them with His light! (Rabbi Chaim Kramer)

"And Yisro, the Priest of Midian, father-in-law of Moses, heard of all that G-d had done for Moses and for Israel, His people..." (Exodus 18:1). Because he was the father-in-law of Moses, he heard and converted. For everything Moses worked to accomplish, during his life and now, after his death, was ONLY to make converts [and bring all humanity back to G-d] (Rabbi Nachman of Breslav, Likutei Moharan 1:215).

In the lessons in Tanya (Ch. 1), it is written: "It should be noted that among the nations of the world there are also to be found those whose souls are derived from *kelipat nogah* [just like Jewish *nefesh ha'bahamis*]. Called 'the pious ones of the nations of the world,' these righteous individuals are benevolent not out of selfish motives but out of a genuine concern for their fellow."

Somebody quotes the Rebbe (Likkutei Sichos, vol. 10, p. 89), "On spiritual terms, they are the holy sparks who are ingrained in *klippah* (impurities) and are yearning to get close to *kedusha* (holiness)."

The Ba'alei Tosfos asks, [Why does the] Talmud [use] the term '*ger shnigyir*'; apparently the proper term should be '*goy shnisgayir*'? To indicate, that the eventual *ger* has a hidden latent Jewish soul which waits to be discovered and activated.

According the Ari, the *geirim* are stray sparks which fell in *klipah* and are restless until they are becoming Jewish. He explains that, this restlessness has to do with Abraham's circumcision, which caused that holy souls belong exclusively to Abraham and not to anyone else (until that point, you could have a holy soul and need not convert as *Meshiselech*, *Mamerei* who had great souls but did not feel an urge to convert).

So, if a holy spark somehow 'fell' into a *goy's* body the holy spark can't rest calmly in his body and has an irresistible urge to become Jewish since Abraham's *milah*, circumcision dictated that all holiness has to be Jewish.

However, this is only about the offspring of Abraham which were post *milah*, but concerning Yishmael, since he was born prior to Abraham's *milah*, therefore, the Ari says, we see so few converts from B'nei Yishmael, since they were not influenced by Abraham's *milah*, so if a stray spark enters them, they don't have the urge to convert."

The Rambam in Igeres Taimon writes that internally, the *goyim* are jealous of the Jews because we were the nation to receive the Torah. The Kli Yakar writes the Esav is jealous of us because he believes Jacob took the blessings from him; and Yishmael is jealous of us because he believes Isaac took his.

However, this doesn't mean that the *goyim* are always going to want to kill us. The sages have told us that anti-Semitism depends largely on our actions, especially in *golus* (exile) because the cause of anti-Semitism is jealousy. It is important to keep a low profile and not draw attention, and to always be aware that we are being judged as Hashem's nation, so make a *kiddush* Hashem (sanctify His Name).

CHAPTER 21:
The Expense of Jewish Living

While a person might be emotionally ready to become Jewish. When they find out the higher living costs, this might give them the final deterrence.

Someone wrote me, "I study and have a vast knowledge of Torah & *Chassidus* but don't keep the laws. I did while I was in the community. Conversion is hard, very hard. It costs not just the process but Jewish life costs more. Add 50% to your shopping & living costs. Its lonely, it's hard to bond to the community even when converted, marriage is difficult."

For this fellow, all the variables overwhelmed him to such an extent that he quit the conversion process. The true reason he quit the process was because his soul indeed did not have a Jewish spark and source. Let's hope that he remains a strong B'nei Noach and doesn't give up on the truth. However, if his soul was to convert, and he dropped it for financial reasons alone, woe to his soul. His soul might have to undergo reincarnation again and another opportunity for conversion will surface.

He brings up some good points about the added costs of being a Jew. *Kosher* food must be inspected by a certified *kosherus* company. This is because of all the additives added to food today, many of which are not *kosher*. *Kosher* meat must go through special slaughtering so that the animal is killed without a pain or suffering. This nearly doubles the cost of your monthly food bill.

If you have children, the added costs are extreme. One

major expense is Jewish private schools. This is one of the largest costs for a Jewish family. While there are scholarships, the schools can't afford to give them out to everyone. If your child needs a special-ed class, they are not always available except for in large cities, and the cost is so much that many are forced to not provide their children with the education they desperately need.

It's nice in theory to say that every child deserves a Jewish education no matter what, but at the end of the day, someone has to pay for that. I was a victim of such a situation, and it was terrible the suffering of being turned away from school because your parents can't afford tuition. Never should this happen to any child. Applying for the scholarships can be demeaning and humiliating. If half of your pay check goes to Jewish schools (if you're lucky), where will that leave you on paying for your rent or mortgage?

Most religious families have a lot of kids, the Torah encourages this. It says that the children are what uphold the entire world.

Keeping *Shabbos* and *Yomim Tovim* (Jewish holidays) are also costly. You have to leave work early on Friday in order to return home for *Shabbos*. Certainly, you can't work on Saturday because you must sanctify the *Shabbos*. There might go your awesome job that you have been working at for years. I remember my mother being harassed by her boss because she had to leave earlier on Friday in order to arrive home for *Shabbos*. They wanted to fire her, and co-workers would often make fun of her for covering her hair and wearing modest clothing.

However, when you serve Hashem, when you believe with all your heart that it is, He that provides, then these obstacles are doable. You believe so much in Hashem that your willing to take upon yourself whatever it takes to be Jewish.

You must accept first before you convert that you will pay $20 for a pack of the same meat that costs your non-Jewish friends just $10. If you think that *Kosher* food tastes better, you have some surprise coming to you. You have to accept that there is no inexpensive fast food sandwich that will melt your belly. During Passover, your food costs will skyrocket. You will spend hours shopping for basic necessities such as *"kosher* for Passover cheese" and *"matzah* crackers", much of which will not be appetizing. You don't exactly hear a bunch of tourists saying, let's go find some *"Kosher* restaurant to have bagels and lox". Jews are only famous for their chicken soup.

Miriam Coyne writes me, "Before I converted, management posted a flyer basically stating that someone took the U.S. Postal Service to court over not accommodating a Seventh Day Adventist to not work on *Shabbos*, Saturday. I'm not sure if they bring in *Shabbos* on Friday evening or not. Then the poster went on to say that he lost his case in court. Now, that did warn me of what I might have to deal with through my career at the U. S. Postal Service.

"I aimed my career to situate myself into a position where it would not inconvenience them by my taking off work on *Shabbos*. Once I got into that position, I just told everyone that I was Jewish, even though I was not yet, because I wanted to see how this would work out. Once I figured it was working, although at times bumpy, I headed onto the more serious part of actively seeking conversion. My rabbi told me that I had to secure a position that would not interfere with *Shabbos* before the rabbis would convert me.

"For the most part of my career, it worked out O.K., it was only when I started getting older and closer to retirement age that management began to play games with my *Shabbos* observance. Every time they tried, I just tried harder with the advice of a rabbi. All the trouble actually strengthened my commitment to Judaism. I felt I was climbing a rocky mountain, but I was able to reach the pinnacle of the mountain. Now that I am retired from the U.S. Postal Service, I am enjoying the spiritual view.

"What surprises will lie ahead for you when it comes to your livelihood, I don't know. However, the path for others has sometimes been fully set and other times filled with thorns. Either way, it will take faith to carry you through all hardships on the road to success. Being prepared and building the tools to overcome them ahead of time, is certainly helpful. However, why assume things will be difficult and have anxiety about it. Your faith has brought you this far, hasn't it?"

CHAPTER 22:
Choosing a Name

A convert is as a newborn child, *k'tinok she'nolad*. A new person chooses a new name for themselves. The rabbis instituted that converts should choose Hebrew names for their new Jewish lives as part of their new identity.

Since the convert is technically considered to be a newborn child, reference to the parent must be of the spiritual parentage adopted by entering into the Covenant of Abraham. There must be a formal label of the conversion that is plainly evident. That is why the convert is termed "*ben* Avraham Avinu, (son of our Father, Abraham)", or "*bas* Sarah Imenu (daughter of our Mother, Sarah)".

Let us take a moment to speak about them in order to appreciate why the convert as well as the Jewish people are so connected to these two figures.

Adam was complete only with Chava. Rashi comments, based on the Midrash, that when Sarah was one-hundred, she was like a twenty-year-old regarding sin. The greatness of a twenty-year-old is her physical strength and idealism. G-d said to Abraham, "Whatever Sarah your wife says, you shall listen." (Genesis 21:12) Sarah had a way of making Abraham feel young; she was enthusiastic and filled with energy. The sages claim that if the woman isn't happy, the husband won't be either. Sarah also had another name - Yiskah, meaning "seer" because she was a prophetess and had the ability to see into the future. Another reason for the name "seer" was that people used to gaze at her beauty. (Talmud Megillah 14a) Sarah was exceptionally beautiful, and all other women, by comparison with her, looked like monkeys

(Talmud, Bava Basra 58a). As beautiful as Sarah was physically, she was even more beautiful in her nature. She was entirely free of sin, and she was exceptionally modest.

In the merit of Sarah, G-d blessed Abraham with wealth (Midrash on Proverbs 31) and with all other blessings. (Tanchuma, Chayei Sarah 4) The greatest blessing for Abraham was that he merited to have Sarah as his wife. As long as Sarah lived, the cloud of glory hovered over her tent, and a light burned from *erev Shabbos* to *erev Shabbos*, and her home was full of blessing.

They were partners in every way. In the Torah portion *Lech Lecha*, we are told that when Abraham and Sarah started out for the Land of Canaan, they brought with them, "The souls which they made in Haran." (Genesis 12:5) We understand this to mean the people they converted to monotheism. Rashi tells us, "Abraham converted the men and Sarah converted the women." (Ibid.)

To summarize, it was mainly Abraham's family that made him blessed and complete. Sarah his wife and son Isaac were his blessings. She brought the *Shechinah* into his home with her devotion to Hashem and her desire to raise Isaac in the path of Hashem. They supported each other in their *chesed* projects and outreach. Alone they wouldn't have been able to accomplish so much but together they changed the world.

The words, אַבְרָהָם זָקֵן, total *gematria* 405 which shares the word שְׁנֵיהֶם *shenahem*, two of them. Even though Abraham was old, he was together with Sarah, and therefore his life had completeness. It was the two of them who made the difference and were parents to the Jewish people. If you take the word בֵּרַךְ *bayrach*, blessed, it totals 222. All are number 2's because blessing doesn't come alone; blessing comes in pairs. (Taken from my Book, Passages of Torah)

People many times choose a name that is similar to their English name, but this is not required. One can choose any Jewish name they desire as there is quite a large pool to pick from. Usually there is one person from the Bible that has inspired the convert to change their entire life, and they choose that name.

One convert of ours, chose my wife's name as she felt eternally grateful that we helped her through her conversion. I guess I shouldn't be offended that she didn't choose my name "Moshe" as one does choose a name according to their gender.

When a person is born, their parents usually name them after a lost relative or after a name they connect to. In this case, it's really special that you personally get to name yourself, so choose what you like. This is one of the most special parts of the conversion process.

The Torah teaches us that the name of a person is their essence. Adam the first man, named all the items on earth and thereby gave them their identity. Inside the name you choose will be your destiny for all time. Therefore, think long and hard before you choose one and go over the reasoning with your rabbi. It is common for Jews to have two names so your welcome to enjoy a second name as well. Whichever name you choose, one thing is for certain, G-d is behind the choice and giving you Divine Inspiration on your choice. It is a very special moment.

CHAPTER 23:
After the Conversion

The *tikkun* and sparks are being gathered up from all types of people. We are seeing a sign that we are getting close to the time of the Messiah's coming since the number of converts to Judaism is at an all-time high. The distance between truth and falsehood is becoming more and more separated. G-d is near to all who call Him, to all who call Him in truth. (Psalms 145:18)

I asked many of my followers who are converts to share with me advice they have for the newly converted. I requested that they share with me both the good and bad. The responses were as follows:

Miriam Metzinger wrote, "Stay in the community where you are most comfortable when converting... don't let anyone pressure you to make any other major life changes in your first year after converting such as getting married or making aliyah... those things can wait until after the first year. Go with your feeling of where you are most comfortable."

Another person writes: "I am happy that I chose Judaism because Judaism is focused so much on the here and now. Human life has value within Judaism. We are expected to build and work on what we have here on this earth. I came from an evangelical Christian past and focusing on life after death was pounded into my mind. There was very little room for thinking about what we should be doing while we are here and/or about the relationships we have to people around us. I am happy that I chose Judaism because Judaism values me. I am happy I chose Judaism because Jews were chosen. We may not always be popular and liked, but that's not important.

What's important is what we are achieving in this world for Hashem." Grethel Jane Rickman, Geulah Bas Avraham Avinu v'Sarah Imeinu

Haddasah Freiberg writes: "I did not know that Jews existed until I was nine. When I moved from Colorado to Chicago, I saw temples and got scared; temples were from the Incas and Aztecs. My mother explained that those were for the Jews, and the Jews originally had the Bible but lost it because they didn't believe in Jesus. I remember thinking if they had it first, wouldn't they know why not to believe in Jesus- why accept a new version?

"When I could rationally wrap my head around the idea of G-d and respect my choice to accept a Divinely created universe (as opposed to a phenomenally impossible series of 'accidents') I wanted to know G-d. The best and closest way to know G-d: become Jewish and learn Torah, do *mitzvos*. Best gift in my life, ever. I won the biggest lottery to ever win."

E. Parone writes: "Since I've converted, I feel like I continue growing Jewishly each day to the point where I say to myself, yesterday I thought I was *frum*, but when I look back, I see how much I have grown, *Yiddishkeit* wise. I see my life as it has been directed from Above because coming from whence, I came, there is no way I could have done so myself. Yes, I may have done my efforts and chose to join 'The Tribe', but I see the Hand Who chose me. I marvel every day at His works and wonders."

Levi Wise says: "It was an arduous and difficult process, but the results are worthwhile."

Ruth M writes: "I was raised as a Catholic, my ancestors were Sephardic Jews. I did not know, nor even dreamed that I had Jewish blood in my veins. Hashem revealed this to me. Little by little His Infinite love and compassion have been leading me to my roots. I am still struggling, but He is way ahead of me in this battle, and I know that whatever purpose He has in my life it will come through. Soon the world will know the truth, and the world will tremble. All I ask in my prayers is for the unity of my people. This is what will bring about the coming of the Messiah."

Margaret writes: "I have never been a leader in a church, but my call has been for over thirty years now. As I have been studying the Tanach, and all related to Judaism, I find myself at home, comfortable. Even though I would have to prove that my ancestors were Jews, but I am thinking about converting. G-d willing. May G-d help me."

An Anonymous person writes: "I feel so close to Him now than ever. He is my Savior, no one else. Hashem is my only G-d."

Someone writes: "I felt like there was something missing always and now there isn't."

Frank Siciliano tells: "When you love your job, you feel like you never work a day in your life," he said. "It's kind of like that."

Camille found answers: "I love the Jewish concept of healing the world and look forward to participating in community service projects."

Batya added: "They embraced us. When we moved, they called to offer a couch or a dresser, anything we needed."

Yossi writes: "My journey was not about answers, but the accumulation of more questions! My search has led to what my heart already knew - Hashem is my hope, my life, and my hope of the world to come. It is my prayer that in my remaining journey I will ever be a light to the nations."

Hannah writes: "For me, converting was the logical step to take, to follow my heart, and finalize my commitment. In my life, there is no greater joy and passion than loving G-d and my fellow Jews"

Moshe writes: "Truly Israel is fortunate to have the Torah of Hashem in their hands to guide them in this dark world of wolves."

Anatasia tells: "My experience has been great. The more that have read about the Jewish religion the more I have learned and understood about life itself."

It says in the Psalms 107:1-32

1. 'O give thanks unto the L-rd, for He is good, for His mercy endureth forever.'

2. So, let the redeemed of the L-rd say, whom He hath redeemed from the hand of the adversary;

3. And gathered them out of the lands, from the east and from the west, from the north and from the sea.

4. They wandered in the wilderness in a desert way; they found no city of habitation.

5. Hungry and thirsty, their soul fainted in them.

6. Then they cried unto the L-rd in their trouble, and He delivered them out of their distresses.

7. And He led them by a straight way, that they might go to a city of habitation.

8. Let them give thanks unto the L-rd for His mercy, and for His wonderful works to the children of men!

9. For He hath satisfied the longing soul, and the hungry soul He hath filled with good.

10. Such as sat in darkness and in the shadow of death, being bound in affliction and iron.

11. Because they rebelled against the words of G-d, and contemned the counsel of the Most High.

12. Therefore, He humbled their heart with travail, they stumbled, and there was none to help--

13. They cried unto the L-rd in their trouble, and He saved them out of their distresses.

14. He brought them out of darkness and the shadow of death and broke their bands in sunder.

15. Let them give thanks unto the L-rd for His mercy, and for His wonderful works to the children of men!

16. For He hath broken the gates of brass and cut the bars of iron in sunder.

17. Crazed because of the way of their transgression and afflicted because of their iniquities--

18. Their soul abhorred all manner of food, and they drew near unto the gates of death--

19. They cried unto the L-rd in their trouble, and He saved

them out of their distresses;

20. He sent His word, and healed them, and delivered them from their graves.

21. Let them give thanks unto the L-rd for His mercy, and for His wonderful works to the children of men!

22. And let them offer the sacrifices of thanksgiving, and declare His works with singing.

23. They that go down to the sea in ships, that do business in great waters--

24. These saw the works of the L-rd, and His wonders in the deep;

25. For He commanded, and raised the stormy wind, which lifted up the waves thereof;

26. They mounted up to the heaven, they went down to the deeps; their soul melted away because of trouble;

27. They reeled to and fro, and staggered like a drunken man, and all their wisdom was swallowed up--

28. They cried unto the L-rd in their trouble, and He brought them out of their distresses.

29. He made the storm a calm, so that the waves thereof were still.

30. Then were they glad because they were quiet, and He led them unto their desired haven.

31. Let them give thanks unto the L-rd for His mercy, and for His wonderful works to the children of men!

32. Let them exalt Him also in the assembly of the people, and praise Him in the seat of the elders.

Chapter 24:
How we can fix the System

Today through DNA testing you can tell if you have Jewish blood in your ancestry. You can even see if you have Jewish cousins and relatives. However, this doesn't prove that your mother is Jewish and her mother. At the end of the day, you can't just blood test your way into Judaism.

It is quite interesting though, how many converts find that they have Jewish blood in them. I've even met some who converted only to find out years later that they were all the time a Jew. We all have our interesting ways in returning to Hashem.

That is what is so sad about the difficulties some converts face. You would think that Judaism, whose entire movement is based on repentance and coming close to Hashem, would exemplify in the *mitzvah* of loving a convert, however, in reality, we have failed.

You must understand, the Talmud explains that the reason the last Temple was destroyed was *sinas chinum*, not respecting one other. As a convert, you might feel singled out in this but really, you're not. If all Jews would respect one another, the Messiah would come immediately.

As with all my books, I always speak about the importance of having *ahavas Yisrael*, loving one another. This especially holds true of the convert. If I were to write a new book specify on loving the convert, who would read it? We Jews already think we are doing enough to love our fellow... Unfortunately, we will keep thinking this until our suffering knocks some sense into us. However, not all hope is lost. There are many good people and communities out there trying to exemplify this important trait. We have to pray to find them and when we can't find them, we must create new havens, not only for Jews but for converts alike.

You can't imagine how many synagogues I have been in and out of over the years, due to their coldness. People can be cold and heartless without even realizing it. Some people are simply shy to new people and it isn't that they personally overlook you. They are busy with their own problems and feel that they have more than enough people around them already. Well enough of the excuses. What can be done about this problem?

Well the solution starts with you. If you know of a convert or someone undergoing conversion, reach out to them and help them to feel like they are a part of your family. If you see a new face in the synagogue, find them a seat and introduce yourself.

Should you be a rabbi at a synagogue. Make it your nature to regularly speak to everyone in your congregation. Stand at the exit door at the end of prayers so that nobody leaves your synagogue without a hearty *shalom*. If you see that nobody is greeting the new folks, then you be the surrogate rabbi, the one to stand at the door to say *shalom*. You have no idea how you can change someone's entire *Shabbos* just from greeting them after prayers.

Put up signs in your synagogue about the importance of *ahavas Yisrael* (loving other Jews). We don't speak about this concept enough. Every year there is a "Chofetz Chaim day" where nobody speaks *loshon hara* and people attend seminars on the subject. There should also be yearly and monthly days for *ahavas Yisrael*.

Everyone has an opinion as to why so many people are suffering from emotional disorders today, however, I'd like to say that so much of this could be fixed if we would just be more loving to others. Friendships seem to be motivated by selfish reasons rather than pure ones. Relationships instead of being a give and take, seem to be just about taking. People expect favors but don't do them back.

We must emulate G-d, and His way is kindness and giving. As you embark on your journey to become Jewish, as an outsider, you will notice the things we overlook and take for granted as Jews. Don't hesitate to point these things out to us. We have been blinded by our own trials and sufferings. You as the new comer, can remind us how pure our souls are. You can remind us of the ultimate goal of life and inspire us to improve.

Rabbi Levi Yitzchok teaches: "There are two types of people who serve G-d. One serves G-d with great intensity but remains by himself and does not attempt to bring others to serve the Creator. Such a person feels that it is enough if he himself worships G-d. There is another type of person, however, who serves G-d, but also works to bring others to serve Him. Such a person emulates Abraham who introduced people [to belief in G-d].

"We find in the writings of the Ari that Noah was punished because he did not try to correct the people of his generation. He was therefore reborn as Moses, and it was for this reason that Moses constantly worked to correct all of Israel."

Our sages speak of one who is, "good to heaven and good to people." (Kiddushin 40a) This refers to the person who serves G-d, but who also tries to bring the irreligious to serve Him. He is "good to heaven" because he serves G-d, but he is also "good to people" because he brings them to serve the Creator.

Noah, however, did not work to bring others to serve G-d... The Torah therefore states that, "Noah walked with G-d." (Genesis 6:9) This means that Noah walked only with G-d. He served G-d by himself, and did not walk with other people, trying to bring them closer to G-d, so that they too should be counted among those who serve Him. (Kedushas Levi, Noah p.8)

CHAPTER 25:
The Heights of the Convert

Rav Zusha once remarked, "When I get to the next world, they won't ask me how I served Hashem compared to another person, they will ask me if I was the best Zusha that I could be." The same is true with the convert. They don't have to compare themselves to other converts or to a born Jew, they have to serve Hashem in their own way. Of course, according to *halacha* (code of Jewish law) to dress and act Jewish, but to also be them self, a unique creation from Hashem.

The Meor Einayim says that the *ohr shebaTorah*, the highest light of the Torah, is not accessible to *gerim*, who are not [biological] children of the forefathers. He says that this deepest level of connection to the Torah, which is beyond its intellectual understanding, is only accessible to Jews who are literal descendants of Abraham, Isaac and Jacob. However, *geirei tzedek*, righteous converts, are unable to attain that same level. This statement is fully cited in the Zohar.

Also, in Parshas Shemos, he teaches about the *ohr*, light, within the Torah. He says that one cannot access this illumination within the Torah all at once. It is only revealed to the person little by little over time.

The Sudilkover Rebbe explained that the explanation is that an *eved*, servant of the King, no matter how intimate his relationship is with the King, will never have the same closeness that the child of the King has. Therefore, there is an aspect of the illumination within the Torah that is accessible to literal children of Abraham, Isaac and Jacob. (B'nei Bechori Yisroel).

He also said that *gerim* are all called "*Tachas Mikanfei*

HaShechina, under the wings of the Divine Presence." However, children of Abraham, Isaac and Jacob are "*l'ma'aleh mi'kanfei HaShechina*, above the wings of the *Shechinah*." Although both are one with the *Shechinah*, they are that way at different "levels" within the *Shechinah*, and therefore the "*Ezrach B'Yisroel*" has access to some higher aspects that the *ger* does not have access to.

All of that being said, the Sudilkover Rebbe continued, "That with *ratzon*, desire, a *ger* can break through that boundary and access the same intimacy with Hashem through the Torah that any other Jew can."

I think we can see this through the history of many great converts and children of converts. Look at the heights reached Rebbe Akiva (ben Gerim), Shemaya v'Avtaliyon (Tena'im), Ben Bag Bag, Ben Hei Hei (also Tena'im) and Onkelus among others. Moshe Rabbeinu (Moses) married a convert, as did Yehoshua.

It is written, "And the Living Angels ran and returned." (Ezekiel 1:14) The soul is carved out of a holy place and should constantly burn to return to its source. In order that it not be annihilated out of existence, it was surrounded by a material body, so that it should also be involved in physical things, such as eating, drinking and business. As a result, it is not constantly involved in worshiping Hashem [and does not become nullified in His Essence].

For this reason, the Emanations (*Sefiros*) have levels of both Greatness and Smallness. [The level of Greatness corresponds to their] "return". [These levels also have their parallel in man.]

When a person has a constant enjoyment, it becomes part of his nature, and is no longer an enjoyment. Man must therefore go up and down in his worship of Hashem. He is then able to sustain the enjoyment which is the main purpose of worshiping Hashem. (Keter Shem Tov 121)

Several merchants were in a strange land. They went off the main highway and could not find their way back. They finally decided that they would rest up and sleep until they could find someone to show them the way to return.

A man eventually came along and gave them directions. This man, however, acted maliciously, and directed them to a place full of robbers and wild animals. Finally, they encountered another individual who led them back to the highway.

The parallel is that the letters of the Torah, with which the world was created, come to this world like merchants in a strange land. They have gotten lost and are sleeping.

When you study Torah for "its sake" you bring these letters back to the highway, attaching them to their root, but when a person does not study for "its sake" he brings them to a place of thieves. (Toldos Yaakov Yosef, Shelach 143c)

This book was just the beginning of your exposure to Jewish life.

"Unlike other faiths, the key to Judaism is study and practice. The only way to get a Jewish 'mindset' is this way, combined with as much exposure to Jewish life as possible." Brachah Devorah bas Sarah

Rebbe Nachman says that when you feel that in *Shamayim* (the Heavens), they are pushing you away and don't want to let you into the gates of holiness, the *ikar* (main thing) is not to be discouraged and not to be afraid. Rather, Hashem is sending that message to you to get you to push harder to be closer to Hashem. (Likutei Moharan 48)

Reb Shlomo Carlebach said, "I want you to know: G-d is opening the gates for the entire world, and the saddest thing is, most people don't even go through the gates.

"You know friends, if we could go back in history, if every person in the world would really live up to their visions, we would be the highest people in the world, the highest. So, you know what the problem is? We believe that G-d can do it, but we don't really believe that we can do it. Why don't we believe that we can do it? Because we think that we have to do it with our own strength, but we don't believe that when G-d give us a vision, He also gives me whatever I need to fulfil it. You know, when someone tells me, 'I have some good advice for you: Go to Israel,' He wants me to buy the ticket. And then he will say, 'I gave him good advice.' You know the way G-d is operating. When G-d tells you, 'Go to Israel,' He also gives you a ticket, but you have to have clear eyes to see it. Some things, G-d is hiding them under the closet.

"You know what Israel needs? If I walk up to the non-religious people and tell them, 'Believe in G-d,' it's sweet, but that is not what Israel needs. I have to walk up to them and tell them, *gevalt* (really) does G-d believe in you, *gevalt* does G-d believe in you. And if they get a taste of that, it will be no problem for them to believe in G-d also."

The Ishbitzer says, "The greatest, highest, deepest, the most glorious G-d revelation is, when G-d lets you know that He needs you." (Open Your Hearts)

If you read this book with an open heart, then I am sure you got the message. G-d needs you to set an example for the world, to be His shining light down here on earth. To make His Oneness known to the world. Now you just have to decide, how deep is your calling from G-d. How can you reciprocate His kindness?

Made in the USA
Coppell, TX
21 December 2020

46812202R00105